HELLO PAT

Other books by the Author

URSULA My Other Life

HELLO PAT

Pat Skinner

Published in 1989 by
The Self Publishing Association Ltd
Lloyds Bank Chamber
Upton-upon-Severn, Worcs

A MEMBER OF

British Library Cataloguing in Publication Data
Skinner, Pat, 1914–
Hello Pat.
1. Great Britain, 1945 –. Biographics
I. Title
941′.085

ISBN 1 85421 080 7

Designed & Produced by The Self Publishing Association Ltd
Printed and Bound in Great Britain by The Eastern Press Ltd, Reading, Berks

For Victor, my first born in England,
who established the roots of my
English family.

PROLOGUE

I was nineteen years old when Hitler became first Chancellor and then the leader, the 'Fuehrer', of all Germans. Within a few years war broke out meaning times of suffering for many thousands of people who were drawn into the maelstrom without being able to understand the reasons for the hatred that consumed the world.

I understood the philosophy guiding the German leadership and I detested it but, like most of my fellow-countrymen, I was a captive of the system. My bourgeois upbringing had not prepared me for struggling against any established regime. 'Leader, you order, we follow' was the slogan of the day, and most of us submitted to that call. Which, in my case, meant having to teach in Poland, Czechoslovakia and finally, in a small village in Austria, settling in peace for a while, away from bombs. I lived there with my four year old son and my war-widowed sister together with her little boy. The story of those years in my life up to the departure for England has already been told.

My knowledge of the English language was very limited. I was able to translate and serve as interpreter in Germany, but I was not at all confident when I had to speak to the people I met in England. Besides, my far from intimate acquaintance with that country had hardly prepared me for the pitfalls I encountered in everyday life. As I wanted to practise my new language I kept a journal during my first years in England. The result is presented here.

Hotel Bellevue, Kiel *15 August 1947*

This is my last evening in Germany, spent in a hotel which was once the stopping place for rich Germans and visitors to the yacht club. Now it is occupied by the British for officers in transit. Dick has gone down to the bar to say goodbye to some of his colleagues. I do not want to go. I need time for myself, time to think. I want to put my thoughts on paper. When I was packing I found this old diary of Dick's, hardly used. It is perfect for what I want.

It is a beautiful summer night, lights twinkle across Kiel Bay, the 'Foerde'. There is a moon. A warm wind caresses my face. Roy is asleep in the room behind me, his dark head snuggled against his teddy. Roy, Dick's son, who from now on is to be my little boy as well.

Yesterday we left the house of a German admiral which had been requisitioned for us, our home for the last six months. We packed all our belongings. I said goodbye to my family earlier on – Marianne, my sister, stoney faced, Mother, only a crisp: "I hope you are doing the right thing", and Father, dear father, hugged me and said: "This is a very big step. Mind you don't stumble". And added: "When we are allowed to travel again and have some money we'll come and visit you." I wonder!

Am I taking the easy way out? Am I, as my mother put it, "One of the rats leaving the sinking ship"? How cruel she sounded when she said that! Did I use British nationality as a convenience to be able to leave my own country? No, definitely not, Dick could have come from anywhere, even from Germany. No, the fact is I am young, in love with a good, reliable man who promises me partnership, erasing memories of a lonely, unhappy marriage.

True, but Henning? Should I stay in Germany for his sake? I am no longer a German and there is no way in which I can fight for my son now. Perhaps there will be, in the future, when my old country will count once more amongst European nations. Klaus, my first husband, married again months ago. Henning is now part of a new family as well, in new surroundings at his father's school. When will I see my son? I last spoke to him a week ago. He was excited that I would be able to send him football boots from England, not a bit concerned that we would not see each other for a long time.

"I won't forget you. I'll send you pictures and lots of letters. I'll be big soon, then I'll come and visit you."

No matter how I try, when I think of him, a feeling of guilt remains.

Dear God, what have I done? Suddenly the full impact of my decisions, taken during the last few months, hits me cruelly. What if I have been wrong about Dick? No, that cannot be. I have known him for two years now, first as an officer amongst several for whom I translated. He was always the most considerate one and, at the same time, unlike others, very hesitant to talk about himself or to enquire into my life. Months went by before we both learned about each other and became friends. And then good friends. But no more than that, for a long time.

It has been a big decision. I must be amongst the first German women to marry an Englishman so soon after the war, and I can understand the doubts my family have. However, I cannot accept the animosity my mother and my sister feel towards Dick who was never involved in the war any more than they were. I cannot forgive them for siding with my first husband and preventing me from taking my eight year old son with me to England. "This is a German child and will be brought up here. There is no more to be said about it."

I bring shame to my family, they tell me. Not only did I marry a foreigner, but also gave up my German nationality for him and for a new life in a country that, until two years ago, had been at war with my people. In their eyes I am not worthy of taking Henning with me.

And there is another crime I am supposed to be guilty of: six months earlier Dick had brought his son Roy, a year younger than Henning, to Kiel. In future, Roy would live with his father, he alone would be responsible for the child. Broken marriages for him and for me – wars do so much more than to destroy houses and kill people.

Dick needed help then.

"Will you come and live with us? Give up your work as an interpreter?" he asked. "The Control Commission will get a house for me. I have already applied for one. I hate seeing you so sad and lonely. I know things will work out for us. We are right for each other. We'll have to wait until my divorce is finally through and then we'll get married."

I smile to myself. What a long, serious speech it was for this quiet man. So honest, too. "I promise, I'll never let you down" he said. I believe him with all my heart.

"And Henning?" I asked.

"What a question," he laughed. "He'll be part of our new family, of course. The children will be brothers."

"It won't be easy for Roy," I hesitated. "He will miss his mother and he remembers the war. He probably hates all Germans."

Dick brushed the thought aside: "Not for long. I feel sure he'll like you. You have such a good way with children."

A few days later I went to talk to my parents about our plans. I shall never forget their reaction. Going to live in sin, as they called it, was bad enough, but eventually marrying an Englishman in the aftermath of the war was unforgivable. They informed Henning's father, shattering my hopes of taking the boy with me. True, I have Roy. I want him to be my son as well, but to leave Henning and head for the unknown . . .

What about Dick's family, though, in spite of their friendly letters? And the many English people I will have to meet eventually, who must at present hate the sight of any German? How will they react? What do they really know about the Germans and Germany? They must have been fed on propaganda, just as we were. Do they realise that there are millions of ordinary peace-loving Germans who did not want any confrontation? Who in the beginning knew very little of the unspeakable atrocities committed by the Nazis? Later, as the war developed, we no longer believed in the Labour Camps we had always been told existed for political prisioners. The rumours, that they were in fact 'KZs', Concentration Camps, where thousands of people died daily, became stronger and more horrific. But most of us kept quiet, hushing up our dreadful suspicions. Too afraid for our own safety. Was that not a crime as well?

Roy and Henning

The events during Hitler's rule were incomprehensible to me; how much more so they must have been to the British.

Will Dick have to suffer because of me? All these thoughts tumble through my mind, confusing, frightening me. Thinking back to the English community we were living in until now, I have no strong reason for fear. Certainly, some families ignored 'the German girl living with that chap', others were friendly and curious about how I coped with Roy, but felt the time was not yet right for social encounters. A few became close friends, disregarding political circumstances, simply treating us as equals. Most of Dick's colleagues came to our wedding reception; one or two stayed away, dissociating themselves from the idea of a 'mixed' marriage. It does not matter to me. These are early days. I understand their feelings.

Dick will be back soon, and I'd better get everything ready for tomorrow, the day I will have to face the English in their country.

19 Hornsey Road, Wood Green *16 August 1947*
In the evening

Roy is asleep, Dick's mother has gone to her sister's house and Dick has informed me that he is going to have a bath.

I listen to the water running. He will be hours. He

likes reading in the bath. It will be good to be alone for a while, to think back to this day, so important for me, and put pen to paper once more.

There were hardly any civilians at Hamburg Airport, and I did not spot a single German. In fact, it was not a proper airport, just a military airfield. Ugly pre-fab huts for the personnel, but nothing for the passengers. The runway and the two planes I could see shimmered in the heat of the summer morning. I felt uncomfortable. I was determined to travel to London in style, which meant wearing the 'Prince of Wales' check suit – made out of one of Dick's old ones – in which I was married a week ago, and a beige felt hat a friend gave me. I wanted to look good to underline the importance of the occasion. Never mind the discomfort. Besides, I have no nice summer dresses.

There is no civilian air traffic in Germany at present, and everybody climbing onto the plane was wearing some kind of military uniform and was speaking English. Dick, Roy and I stood on the runway for a long time, saying very little. It was too hot and dry to do anything.

I looked at Dick. What was he thinking? Was he concerned about the reception I would get in London? Yes, but was he as apprehensive as I was? He has taken on a big responsibility. He seemed very self-assured and directed his attention once more to the fuelling of the plane, totally absorbed in the technicalities of the procedure, trying to explain it to Roy. For a moment I resented the closeness between them. I felt lonely and so bruised. They were both coming home,whereas I was leaving my whole familiar world behind. And yet, in my heart I knew he behaved like that because he has no doubts about our decision. He is convinced that for us to start a new life together is the right thing to do. And he does not expect me to have any doubts either. Why should he? Spring had been beautiful for us. Roy has begun to accept me. Above all, Dick and I love each other.

At last it was our turn to board the plane. We were the last ones in. All three of us felt the impact of the event. The plane was half empty. Roy sat by the window and I took the seat between him and Dick. Eventually, we took off. It was Roy's first flight and, on leaving the ground, he pulled the curtains across the window very decidedly and shut his eyes. I felt like doing the same.

"I am frightened too, you know?" I said, gripping his hand.

Apart from a five-Reichsmark flight over Stettin during an air-display before the war, I have never flown. Dick's remark that take-off is always the most dangerous moment because of all the fuel on the plane did not exactly help. How like him to concentrate on cold facts to hide any emotional concern.

And I allowed myself to go back to my thoughts. I thought of the future, the distant future rather than the immediate one. Dick and I know that for me, to be a wife and a mother alone would not satisfy me totally. After a while, when we are settled, I would like to work in England: translate, teach perhaps. Yes, go back to teaching as I had done during the war. What great sense of achievement it gave me then to be somebody in my own right, not just the teacher's wife who belonged in the house. But teaching German? I laugh to myself: who at the present time would want to learn that language? We'll see. If not German, then perhaps French. I am aware of the needs of a family, but I have my own needs too, and Dick and I met and fell in love on those terms. We know it will be an adventure, a dangerous one. But aren't all marriages?

I kept trying to convince myself that this was the journey of no return. If I started it and, at the same time, secretly dreamt of going home I'd be lost.

I may return to Germany one day, but the people and places I know there will have changed, and I shall have changed as well. Perhaps I will – some time – see the friends and relatives I have loved again, hear my own language around me once more, but it can never be the old home-country. There are the shadows of the past, too, shadows of crimes which might have happened somewhere else, but did not. They were committed by my people. From now on I belong neither to the conquerors nor to the conquered. Housman's words flashed through my mind then: "I, a stranger and afraid, in a world I never made." But why the misgivings? It is up to me to shape the new beginning, to grow roots again, helped by the man I married. I forced myself to look out of the window, took a deep breath and argued: "Alright now. That is enough of doubts and fears. This is going to be a new life, filled with trust and love. Together we must succeed."

Besides, I was coming to the country I have liked so very much since my student days. What would my beloved English teacher think about me now if she were alive? We kept in touch corresponding for many years. She knew Britain intimately and spent most holidays in some part of it. She believed in democracy, she admired Churchill's qualities as a leader during the war, and she paid for that with imprisonment and death. She had not simply been a teacher to me, she had been a paragon. She made me read English literature and implanted a love which could only grow when, as a student, I visited London for the first time in 1936. I stayed with a family so unlike any German middle-class family I had ever known, that my reaction after a few days was I could happily live in this country. There was 'partnership' in the house of my hosts. Partnership of the kind Dick has talked about.

Gradually the flight was becoming exciting. There, way down, was the war-torn landscape of Germany, slowly disappearing in the haze of the August heat, giving way to the canals and green pastures of Holland and then to the Channel, glittering in the bright sunshine.

Any minute now, the coast of England. I gazed out of the window. I did not want to miss that moment. And I had to overcome any negative feelings or fears.

The famous white cliffs of Dover stood out glaringly, stark in the bright sunlight, so different from the gently curving Baltic coast, crowned by pinewoods. Where was 'this green and pleasant land', though? The fields spreading out below us looked brown and dusty from the air, the earth cracked. Where were the rich green meadows I remembered from my visit to England over ten years ago? Where were the trees and shrubs in their glory, from brilliant green to bluish shades? And the cornfields? I felt let down. A dream picture had been destroyed.

Dick's mother had written to us that the country was suffering, rather than enjoying, an extremely hot, dry summer. And for once it has been possible to plan for weeks ahead without much fear of rain. But I was disappointed.

Not long before I was able to see the millions of London chimneys from the air. How ugly they looked! I have never seen anything quite so dull and regimented. In 1936 I arrived in London by train. Liverpool Street Station was very impressive then. But if all these chimneys were smoking in winter . . . I began to understand why people talk about the London pea-souper.

We landed at Northolt. I was very tense. No, more than that: frightened. Just over two years ago this was enemy country, and now I want to live here. Surely, I look different from the people around me? Can they see I am German? I gripped Dick's hand and tried to smile at Roy.

"Don't worry," Dick said. "You'll be fine." And squeezed my hand.

"Worry, I am not worried. I am petrified, panic-stricken! Everybody seems to look at me!"

"Rubbish," he said in his usual matter-of-fact manner. "They look at you because you are pretty and they think, 'how on earth did that ordinary-looking fellow find such a good-looking wife and son'?"

Then there were the formalities to come. I felt very conscious of my brand new British passport. No need for that; a pleasant young customs officer looked at it, gave me a big smile and said "I hope you will be very happy here."

Dick put his arm around me.

"There," he laughed, "welcome to England." And an impatient Roy tugged at my side. All he wanted was to see Grandma, of course.

An airport bus took us along the Great West Road,with factories everywhere, all intact, and on to the terminal in Cromwell Road. Then a real London taxi. How I longed to ride in one of those when I was a student in London. And how I always wondered at their odd square appearance. The driver piled up our luggage by his side. "Why there? Isn't there a boot?" I asked.

Dick tapped on the partition to attract the driver's attention, who slid it back.

"Yes, gov?"

Dick just wanted to chat to the taxidriver. He felt at home again. I would have liked to say something, but although my English is more or less fluent, I dreaded the question "Where are you from?" An accent would shine through, even if it is not of the grating German kind. So, I only listened and was very pleased I understood what they were saying.

Wood Green at last. The house where my new mother-in-law lives. I felt sick, got out of the taxi and avoided looking at people in the street. Somebody stopped and stared at me. At us or at me? "Don't be silly" I told myself. It is a modest little road. Just glancing along the street, I realised how small the houses were, all in a row, some of them badly in need of a fresh coat of paint. Not many people would use taxis here; that was probably the reason for the stare. But it did not help. Not really.

Dick's mother had been waiting for us, possibly behind the curtains, because the moment we pulled up, the door of the two-up-two-down house opened.

"Grandma!" Roy threw himself into the arms of an elderly lady with a kind, tired face. She looks younger than my mother, with iron-grey hair, her eyes hidden behind thick-lensed glasses. I know from Dick that she can only see very little. Everything is so neat, from her little white apron over a blue dress to the room behind her.

"We've brought our new Mummy", Roy reported.

I looked at her and she smiled. Letting Roy go she turned to me and said, "Hello, Pat. Welcome, my dear." Dick had often written to her about me and she had always called me 'Pat' in her letters to him. "What beautiful hair you have, let me look at you."

She led us through the little hall into a large kitchen with an old-fashioned iron range which, over the years, has been lovingly black-leaded. The table by the bow window was laid with bread and butter, jam, biscuits and a large iced cake with 'welcome' written on it.

"I didn't expect that," I stuttered timidly. "I don't know what to say."

"Nothing," she replied. "You are part of the family now and you *are* welcome."

And then she brought a big pot of coffee. She thought I might like this better than tea. 'Germans prefer coffee.'

Afterwards I was convinced that good English tea would have been better. Her coffee had been made with milk. She is definitely not a coffee expert. I'll make sure I say I prefer tea next time, I like the way they make tea here.

"Make this your home for a while," my mother-in-law said, "until you have decided where to go from here. Think of it as a holiday. Let Dick show you London as he knows it. I'll stay at my sister's; she lives only a few minutes away."

"Yes, Dick has told me already. Why can't you stay here as well?"

"Ah," she laughed, "there will be no room for me."

She showed me into the bedroom. What about the rooms upstairs? I was confused, but did not say anything. I did not talk for quite a while after that, but simply held my breath. The bedroom was dark, dingy, altogether awful, though spotlessly clean. A huge wardrobe, a large double bed, a dressing table and a window looking out onto a small, rather neglected patch of lawn.

And the bed! I have never slept in a double bed before. I can see great problems. Dick is so much weightier than I. I would always end up rolling towards him. And what if one of us had a cold? Or flu? Or did not feel like having the other one close? Practical considerations these; love does not come into it. Still, I do not want to hurt him. He has known double beds from his early days. It would be difficult for him. I will have to talk seriously about this with my husband sometime.

"There is a small room here for Roy. We call it a box room." She showed it to me. "And a lodger in one room upstairs. I need the money. He's nice and quiet. You won't notice him at all."

Now I understood. But why was I complaining? Have I not slept in barns and fields on the long walk from Austria to North Germany? Then, after the war, did I not share the same room with six people, all my family, for months and months? One room for waking, sleeping, cooking, washing? This was paradise compared to those conditions. Anyway, it is only meant for a short time. But I am determined to sleep in my own bed once we have a home of our own.

After we unpacked we went for a walk through Wood Green High Street. The area seems to be a working class district, but everyone was well dressed this Saturday afternoon and loaded with weekend shopping. There were crowds of people around; buses and cars made it difficult to cross the road. For years I have not seen so many cars – how empty Kiel is in comparison.

Strange, the great number of women in bright pinks, blues, pastel shades. With colourful hats, too. At home thousands and thousands of women wear black still, and will probably wear it for years to come. During the war they were even issued with special clothing coupons for buying black clothes, to show they were in mourning. These people in England are right, though. I am sure there are many women amongst them who have lost husbands, sons, brothers in those terrible years behind us, and yet, advertising grief by wearing black will not bring anyone back.

The shops seemed full of goods of all kinds, and food. Do they really have food rationing here? I know they do. But in Germany the shops are still empty, with the exception of one or two days in a week when people push around for their meagre rations which are not always obtainable, even though advertisements say so.

"I'd like an ice cream please, Pat." Roy does not call me 'Mummy'. Not yet.

An ice cream? How marvellous! "Can we? I mean, can

one just buy them?" I cannot believe it. I can hardly remember what they are like.

"Sure. Come on!" Roy did not even notice my surprise.

"But I haven't got any money." I said "Let's ask Daddy."

We had lost him for a moment. Ah! He was looking at motorbikes in a shop, his old love.

"Can we have ice creams, Pat and I? She has no money. Didn't you give her any?"

Dick grinned. "I suppose I have to, eventually. Here you are."

I looked at the coin: half a crown. That complicated British currency. I remembered it so well. I handed it to Roy.

"Go on, then. You get them, and bring the change, please."

Roy ran off, and Dick winked at me.

"That was clever. Are you perhaps just a little afraid? On Monday you will go shopping with me, my girl."

It is so easy to call Dick's mother 'Mum'. There was instant acceptance on both sides. She left us to settle in, with a shy plea of "be kind to each other" and "I think Dad would have liked you, I'm sure." She would never interfere. No fear here of a 'wicked' mother-in-law. She did not, for the time being, refer to Nazis either. That is a relief.

This afternoon she talked of Uncle Otto, a German carpenter, who settled in England before the First World War and married into the family. And of his compulsory registration during the war, with regular visits by police officers who eventually became his good friends. All this in a quiet, tolerant way. No bitterness towards Germans, generally. I am very grateful.

Wood Green *25th August 1947*

During this first week we have stayed here in Wood Green I have been handed round. I have met Auntie Rose, Auntie May, some cousins of our own age, Dick's first wife Peggy and her family. She had helped me in Kiel by sending many useful parcels with clothes.

I overheard Peggy's mother on the telephone: "She is very nice, you know. Thank goodness she speaks English . . . oh yes, very pretty and, I think, good fun . . . Yes, alright . . . yes, come round now, have a sherry with us."

I grinned. Peggy looked at me, very apologetically. "I'm sorry. I suppose mother thought you wouldn't understand."

"I don't mind", I laughed. "In any case, she was very complimentary."

Very much so. To be good fun, to have a sense of humour is, in the English mind, very high praise indeed.

And the lady who rang earlier appeared. She surveyed me thoroughly, greeted me with a carefully pronounced, "How do you do?" and was surprised when I answered in a much faster voice, "How d'you do? It's a pleasure meeting you," which left her slightly breathless.

"Pat, this is wicked," I said to myself, but couldn't help getting a certain amount of satisfaction out of my naughtiness.

Everybody has to have a good look at me. Everybody wants to say "Hello, Pat." Ursula (that is my real name) no longer exists. She belongs to my past life. She was left behind in Germany. When Dick and I first met and he asked about my Christian name, he was appalled to hear it was Ursula. He used it, just the same, until much later he gave me the name he liked best for the woman he was going to marry: Pat.

There is a great deal of curiosity about me, yes, but not the resentment I expected. Perhaps I am very alien to them? Nobody in the family has travelled further than France. Australia some of them know, but that is different: people speak English there. France and Germany mean Europe. I am confused. Surely, England belongs to Europe? I feel as if I have come from a different planet.

One or two of the relatives spoke in a very loud, slow voice to me when we met and were surprised that I answered fluently. They heaved a sigh of relief, hugged me and laughed: "Thank goodness, you are one of us. We didn't know what to think."

It seems, not only have I found a husband, but acquired a close-knit family as well. And slowly I am losing the feeling of mistrust that had bothered me in the beginning. People are genuinely friendly, I think, and the family is sincerely concerned about our new life.

So far I have heard only a few courteous, slightly distant, 'How do you do's,' I was taught to use a long time ago. 'Hello' in Germany is only used on the telephone. It seems to me such an easy, friendly greeting, coupled with a firm handshake. No handshake though, on leaving. Something I only remember when I stand there, hand out-stretched, waiting for a response. Of course, that is reserved for serious 'Goodbyes', not to be used in cases of 'See you soon' or 'Come again' which nearly everybody says in such a case.

"It must be nice at work," I remarked to Dick when we returned from a visit to a friend's house yesterday. "Not to go round an office every morning and evening shaking hands with lots of colleagues. It makes life much more comfortable. And I like these Sunday morning invitations just for a drink. So informal."

"You wait until Christmas. It's open house in many families."

"Will we do that?"

"I hope so, especially the first Christmas in our own home."

Oh yes, this will be the next big thing to happen: looking for a house. Life is going to be fun. Difficult at times no doubt, but fun.

Wood Green *30 August 1947*

I have been meeting many kind people. They are obviously a little inquisitive ('let's see what his German wife is like'), and often very forthcoming in offering advice of various kinds. But not only advice, between them, friends and relatives have sufficient clothes coupons for me to acquire a 'New Look' suit.

After all the austerity of the war years women want to be glamorous once more; the desire for a little dash is very strong. The 'New Look' gives them their chance. It means full skirts as against the tight, short, material-saving ones; tiny waists; some frills even; elegant, high-heeled shoes made of real leather. No more clomping around for me in clumsy shoes with wooden soles. Dick has bought me a cream linen suit and a thin, lacy jumper to go with it. That, together with the 'real imitation pearls' he has given me makes me feel like a queen. And everything made of such good materials, no mixture with wood fibres here. German skirts and trousers used to shrink in wet weather.

Can anyone imagine what it feels like to go and buy something absolutely new to wear? I have my own coupons as well. They can be saved for winter clothes. I dream of a warm woollen coat, tartan skirts and twin sets. Perhaps I can have a pretty party-dress for the winter as well, if I am careful with my coupons? No, I don't have to be. Fibre-glass materials, for curtains mainly, are 'free'. Beautiful, multicoloured patterns, just right for an evening dress. I'll bear that in mind.

31st August 1947

A first coach outing to the seaside: Southend on a Sunday. It is about thirty-five miles to the sea, a very straight journey, taking three-quarters of an hour. We stopped close to the coast in a large car park full of coaches, took our picnic basket and towels and walked down to the beach. I gasped. I was appalled, but dared not show my reaction to Dick and Roy. The incoming tide looked inviting, wonderful, the beach is wide and fairly clean though obviously, thousands of Londoners come here on Sundays. But the noise! Blaring music everywhere, ice cream stalls, the smell of chips, eaten out of newspapers, people everywhere, sitting on harbour walls or the promenade, standing around in groups, fully decked in funny paper hats, some licking pink fluffy clouds of candy floss . . . It was too much for me.

A group of children were watching a Punch and Judy show. I stopped for a moment. I liked that. We had puppet shows in Germany, but in theatres and at fairs, not on the beach. And there were children on donkeys, riding along close to the edge of the water. I looked at the long pier and felt guilty. Comparisons kept intruding: a pier, reaching out into the Baltic, was a solitary place, beautiful to walk along on a summer evening, to watch a sunset and see the fishing boats going out into the night. But Southend is full of roundabouts, cafés with loud music and stalls displaying cheap, dubious picture postcards. I was deeply disappointed. Roy revelled in all the turmoil around him; I am sure Henning would react like that as well. For a second I shut my eyes and could see both boys together. I could hear not only Roy's voice, "Let's have a look here" and "Can I have sixpence to go on the big wheel?" but also my own son's shrieks of delight.

I hated all the noise, and, waking from my dreams, managed to say: "How awful! Is it like this everywhere at the seaside?"

"No," Dick said, "you wait. I'll show you beautiful quiet places, rocky shores and deep bays. Be patient. Don't forget, this is close to London. Many people come here just for the day, away from the big city. They have their own way of enjoying themselves. You wait until I show you Devon and Cornwall."

I tried to fight my disappointment and force myself to think clearly. They are a different kind of people. They love doing things together, they like to be in a crowd. As they are in a pub. Who am I to judge?

"Perhaps we can walk a bit further away from the masses?" I suggested this to Dick.

"Why not?" he answered, and we left the scene and the noise, so ugly to me, behind, much to Roy's disgust.

There seemed to be people like myself who wanted to enjoy the beach and the sea. We walked along the water, carrying our sandals, and then stopped at a quiet place.

"Now," and I opened our big beach bag, "who is for a swim and then for something to eat?"

The tide was fully in, all three of us are good swimmers. We changed quickly and raced down to the water. It was marvellous! And how salty! The Baltic is not tidal and does not taste so bitter and salty as this. It was simply wonderful! To think that Great Britain has thousands of miles of coast. Will I really see some of it? Dick has promised. I love swimming and walking along the shore.

We came out of the water, and I had to stop myself laughing: a group of fathers was playing cricket on the beach with their children.

Didn't they look funny! They were in long shorts (similar to the ones worn by English football players), some had rolled up their trousers, with exposed braces, and some were wearing handkerchiefs on their heads to protect themselves against the sun.

The mothers in flowered dresses, cardigans across their shoulders, very solemn, were sitting quietly watching or knitting. They probably understand the game, whereas it will take ages for me to even try to. It seems so complicated! And it is unknown in Germany.

The seaside I knew had been so different. We used to hire a high-backed wicker beach chair, with a hood, for the duration of our stay. The seat is lockable to safeguard the clothes, the hood can be adjusted according to the position of the sun. Having chosen a place for this chair, the family promptly start to build a wall around it, thereby establishing proprietorship of the area enclosed by the sandwall. This is standard practice; everybody respects each other's claim. Well, nearly everybody: in cases where somebody trespasses on somebody else's property, loud, even warlike encounters are the result. Why does that begin to appear absurd and ridiculous to me?

4 September 1947

Yesterday, Uncle John – Auntie May's husband – was on the phone to Dick. We arranged to meet him today at lunch time at the *Captain's Cabin,* in central London. Uncle John is an insurance executive in the City.

We arrived there at about one, but Uncle John was a little late. This pub has a nautical flavour. I've been to pubs before, but they were different. Each seems to have a character of its own. In all of them it appears as if the renowned reserve the English are supposed to have is left at the door. The atmosphere can be quiet, but is convivial and usually leads to casual chats at the bar.

At the *Captain's Cabin* there were young office workers, some with and some without girls, a few City gents in dark suits and bowler hats – but no umbrellas on this warm sunny day – some people sitting in corners hidden behind newspapers.

Yes, it must be because everybody goes to the bar to get drinks that it is so friendly. No service at the tables. If you feel like talking you tend to 'prop up' the bar.

I was nervous. Did I look alright in my new beige dress, with the high-heeled red sandals Dick bought for me? I did so want to please him and my new uncle. I knew that Uncle John was educated at a Public School. During my few weeks in London before the war I had had no contact with people like that. To me 'Public School' meant money, Eton or Rugby, aristocracy, and some decadence. It also meant brilliant lecturers and talkers to many of whom Communism is something of a mental exercise. I also know that this new uncle is a much-travelled man, that he and his wife have a beautiful house in Purley and that their daughter is studying to be a teacher. What would they think of me?

A moment later I realised I need not worry. There he was, a tall lanky Englishman, a wide mouth, clean shaven, smoking a pipe, his face breaking into a big smile.

"Hello, Pat, I've already heard a lot about you. Do you think you'll like it here? I hope you'll be very happy."

No mention of my past. None of Dick's relations has, so far, referred to the war or my personal problems either. What does the silence mean? They must want to talk about it. Do they sense my apprehension of the subject? Are they trying to ease me into their way of living without upsetting me? I hope so. I am not ready to discuss recent German history nor talk to them about Henning. I am still too involved, feeling the pain of leaving him behind every night when I read a story to Roy and tuck him up.

We sat down with beer and a pie.

"Not bad, is it?" he said.

Some English story flashed through my mind. Food in Public Schools – so I had been told in that story – was the worst in the country. Anything had to be better than that. I did not say anything. I liked the beer I drank, not the pie I ate. I know a little about English people easily accepting food in a restaurant which Germans would send back without hesitation. An egg for breakfast which is too hard or too soft, a soup that is not hot enough. No German, having to pay for it, would say 'thank you' for that.

But, oh, Uncle John is nice. "May and I are going to Sweden to visit old friends. How about staying in Purley? We'd like someone to look after the house, and your Mum could have her home back again."

There, he referred to the immediate future, for the moment much more important than the past.

"Well, yes," we said.

"What are your plans, anyway? Are you going back to your old firm, Dick?"

"Yes, they'll have me back. But I don't want to start before October. I'd like to give Pat some time to get used to things."

How like him. Considerate, anxious to give me a good start.

"You must come over on Sunday, with Roy. Meet May. You said you are interested in the theatre. Well, you'll have a lot to talk about, she loves it too."

It is true. We have a lot in common. Auntie May is a lovely old lady, bright-eyed and amusing, occasionally breaking into a quite girlish giggle. She was a leading light in local amateur operatics, a soprano that sounds a bit croaky now. She introduced me to 'Music Hall' which I had never heard about.

Amateur theatre? Apart from religious plays performed by church groups and rather crude comedy played in some parts of Germany by amateurs, in Bavaria and the Rhineland for example, there is no such thing in Germany. And here is a delightful old character performing – with some restrictions – the cancan to my accompaniment on the piano. My playing is pretty restricted too. I am not used to 'performing' that type of music and rattling it off on the piano is a major task for me. They applauded and I knew then that I would simply *have* to have a piano one day and play and play as I have loved to do in the past.

My thoughts go back to the summer of 1945 when, one night, we had found some shelter in a half burnt out vicarage. An elderly lady invited us in. Looking around, my eyes focussed on an unfaded rectangular patch on the wall. That was, no doubt, where Hitler's picture had hung. I could not help thinking how naive it was not to disguise the absence of the painting. How often during the last weeks had I seen such an empty place on a wall.

But then I caught sight of something much more

important: "Oh, you have a piano," I called out. "How lucky it was not ruined."

"Yes," the lady replied. "My husband used to play. Do you play? Would you like to? Please, nobody has used the instrument for a year now. Nobody, since he was killed."

I sat down, my hands idle on the keys. Could I still play? My rough brown hands. But it was as if they suddenly took on a life of their own and played. The first chords of Beethoven's Moonlight Sonata – would I remember it all? The music filled the miserable little room, it carried me away as it had always done. And then the tears came. Music like this was eternal. Our whole desperate situation did only mean one tiny phase in our existence. It would pass, it had to.

May said something, and I turned away from old, haunting memories. If I can join some local amateur company once we are settled . . . My old dream of acting has never quite died.

Purley looks nice and there is such beautiful country around it. But, before deciding whether to accept Uncle John's offer, we went to see Auntie Rose. She would like us to stay with her as well.

She is lovely. A big, warmhearted woman with a large family. I met her a few days ago. She and her husband own two public houses, one in Wood Green and one in the country. I was appalled that same evening to see so many children outside the big corner pub while their parents spent the evening inside, drinking and joining in the songs the pianist bashed out on the keyboard. I know children are not allowed into a public house. They are probably quite used to it on a Saturday night. On that occasion there were, however, even babies in prams watched over by an older brother or sister, and I did not like it at all.

Auntie Rose is the eldest of the three sisters, much quieter than May, with lined features and a warm, vibrant voice. She is very much the business head of the family, her husband suffering from ill-health. I am told she owns a beautiful old house on the Essex coast, in Walton, where year after year during the summer months members of the family gather. And not only the family: any friend who has been ill, who cannot afford a holiday, who badly needs a break by the sea – they are all welcome. Sometimes there are as many as twenty people in the house. All bring their ration cards although I do not know that anybody ever pays anything. But then: two public houses means money in the family.

She is an ardent conservative, a staunch supporter of Churchill and, very early on, talks of the need to reconstruct Germany, even though the past events in my old country are as incomprehensible to her as they must be to most British people.

"We cannot have a desert in the middle of Europe," she repeatedly says. "The Russians would love it and move straight in."

Conversations like that strengthen my optimism and give me growing confidence in some kind of future for Germany. And yet, they are bewildering as well:

"The horror of war is succeeded by the tyranny of peace," she exclaims, quite dramatically. "I don't know who said it, I read it somewhere, and it's true."

And my mother-in-law, forever loyal to her sister, joined in:

"Quite right. If Winnie were still here, we would not have to put up with meat like this," pointing to a scraggy looking bit of beef on her plate. "He would have seen to it that beef is tender and that we get decent lamb, not only mutton."

I wonder. For twelve years, in Germany I had known only one political party and had feared it. The freedom of choice in German elections was something I had heard my parents talking about, in whispers, at a time when there existed only one political party, the NSDAP. I was too young to vote in 1933, but I remember still.

People were given two ballot papers, one white, the other one green. The white paper asked you to vote for Hitler as Chancellor – no alternative offered – the green one posed questions, such as:

'Do you endorse the policies carried out by your Government? Do you solemnly pledge it your support?' You were wise to put your cross behind these questions and not to write down any adverse criticism. There were spies everywhere.

I like England as it is. Never mind the thirteen ounces of meat and six ounces of butter everyone is entitled to per week, never mind the South-African snoek people grumble about. There are quite a few items of food that are 'free' and vegetables are plentiful and fresh. And, if you are really desperate there is, for Londoners, always Petticoat Lane Market on a Sunday morning, where moderate black marketeering helps fill the shopping bag. I admire the idea of a welfare state and try to understand the misgivings Dick's family have. True, when Winston Churchill left the Government in 1945, millions of people must have felt deserted and bewildered. Had he not won the war for them? Or, could it be that his strength had been for *war,* not for peace? The nation perhaps sees the dawn of an even braver and newer world. I would think the present one is complicated enough!

However, six years of danger and discomfort, in part standing alone against a world of enemies, had left the British desiring a change. Maybe with less strength at the top? People made themselves believe in incredible promises, and Churchill's Government was swept away by a great majority. Auntie Rose went as far as saying:

"If only Churchill had taken the lead of the Labour Party, I'm sure we would be alright now."

I then asked her about the Liberals, to which she replied that they were only invented to split the votes. I feel very ignorant indeed.

Auntie Rose showed me a flag, a Union Jack, made of

pure silk. It looks very fragile. What is curious is that it has a very stern looking Queen Victoria in the Centre. She explained that flags like this once were distributed to the population at the time of Queen Victoria's Diamond Jubilee, back in 1897. People were asked to display them on their balconies or in their windows. Her parents had this particular one. There is history behind it and somewhere, deep down, a sense of belonging.

I must have shown a lot of admiration, for in the end she gave the flag to us. I am very pleased. Dick looked amused. He will frame the flag, but simply to please me. I am not at all sure he wholeheartedly agrees with his aunt.

September 1947

We have moved to Purley. It looks prosperous, with pleasant suburban houses, lovingly cared-for gardens, quiet residential areas away from the traffic and noise of a very good shopping centre. May and John's house, which is full of beautiful old, well-kept furniture, is a haven. Now I have to be an English housewife, look after my two men and, for a few weeks, take good care of the house.

I wonder about Dick's family. What a mixture they are and, in spite of that, so close. John and May, professional people; Auntie Rose and her husband, wealthy publicans; one brother successful in Australia; and my mother-in-law all her life limping behind. She had married a brass founder. She herself had been an accomplished florist until she injured her eyes in an accident. To cure a chronic bronchitis of Dick's father they emigrated to Australia where Dick grew up. Father could not be cured. Furthermore, they were homesick and so returned and found all the help they needed from the family. When Dick's father died, the family rallied round and helped with Dick's further education. I thought of my mother's sister, Aunt Ida, in my own family. Always the black sheep: marrying 'beneath' her, divorced and remarried, smoking cigars. Nobody helped her; instead it was always: "When you are in Kiel, there is no need to visit Aunt Ida. She is not really one of us."

1 October 1947

We have started looking for a house. It should not be too far away from Dick's engineering firm, with a suitable school nearby for Roy.

We want it in a quiet area. I have learnt a lot during these first few days of house hunting: Rates? Semi-detached? Detached? Freehold? Leasehold? All these terms are new to me.

How much simpler to rent a flat and, if later on it became necessary, exchange flats with another party. But when I said what I thought to Dick, he did not agree with me: "Perhaps simpler, but not at all the ideal solution in this country. People want to *own* their homes. They may pay for twenty-five years to achieve this, but brick by brick it becomes theirs. For their children or for future years when they are too old to work and earn." Yes, I remember the famous saying: 'My home is my castle'.

I thought of that cliché when I first wandered along streets and saw rows and rows of small houses, each with a fence or hedge round the garden. A castle, with your own front and back entrance, with a garden that belongs to you alone, not just to be looked at by a number of tenants and cared for by the Landlord's gardener (that is, if there is a garden at all). No longer the affluent and the poorer ones in one building, where the back – for the poor – overlooks dingy yards with dustbins, in a city of tenants, as I had known all my life.

Perhaps buildings would be different in Germany now. There would be so much space once the rubble of the war had been cleared away. I remember how I had envied the few girls at school whose parents owned houses. I also remember my mother's incredulous voice, shortly before we left for England: "He'll buy a house? What else has he told you? He is not even an academic." So different from this reality here.

We have approached estate agents to find a suitable house for us. I can hardly translate the words into German! I do not know any Germans who have bought a house and I am quite unfamiliar with the procedure. Then, to complete a contract, solicitors are involved to negotiate the purchase. We become one link in a chain of people buying and selling property. If we are unlucky the chain breaks through one deal not being carried out, and we virtually have to start all over again.

Once more I ask myself the old question: why go through all that trouble? Actually, I know the answer by now. I even begin to understand it. It is to possess a home, not simply to rent it. It is to have a castle of one's own.

Panic! A garden? I love flowers, but know very little about growing them. My family never had a garden. Beautiful geraniums on a balcony, cyclamen and hyacinths between the double windows, always cut flowers in the flat, that was the extent of my horticultural experience. I have been totally uninterested in botany until now, but realise already that the people I have met so far grew up knowing so much more about plants and their botanical names than I would ever know. Do they all understand Latin or Greek? Of course not, but how easily they use names like antirrhinum, cyclamen, nasturtium where – in Germany – I would call them lion's mouth, alpine violet and capuchin cress. And I think a similar fact applies to medicine. In Germany poliomyelitis is children's paralysis, pneumonia to the ordinary people is inflammation of the lungs, and only the medical profession uses the Latin names. Ah well, there are a great many things I have to learn.

34 Geneva Gardens
Chadwell Heath *17 November 1947*

We moved into our first home yesterday. It is a nice, three-bedroomed, semi-detached house with a long, narrow garden which was full of roses when we looked at it first. Then Dick had remarked: "That'll be easy for us," he is not a passionate gardener, "roses are not difficult to grow and they keep most weeds away." It looked wonderful to me but, on moving in, we found that the previous owners had taken all the roses with them. I was furious.

"How could they? We bought the house and the garden from them!"

"Alright," Dick tried to calm me down. "It was not very nice, but they are entitled to it."

I am disappointed in a whole nation.

The house looks inviting, friendly, with open fires everywhere, which is the norm here. Would we have to carry coal upstairs to have warm bedrooms? I shudder and refuse to think about that. This problem has to be Dick's, not mine. Perhaps we can have electric fires instead?

I had grown up with central heating, with big, rather clumsy looking radiators filled with water in every room. There was always a huge boiler and masses of coal in the cellar of the block of flats, and a caretaker saw to the heating system.

I look at the windows as well, very suspiciously. Pretty flimsy, not tightly closing. No double glazing. I think back to Stettin: In winter, there were flowering plants between the double windows, giving cheer and colour. In summer, the inner windows were taken out and stored in the cellar, and outside blinds protected us from too much sun.

I hope we shall be warm in our new home. War memories of feeling cold are far worse than of being hungry. I never want to be without hot water and warmth again.

18 November 1947

I think we ought to do something about Roy's room. It is mainly pink, dreadful for a boy. I asked Dick whether he knew where we could find a decorator and if we could afford one.

"Yes and no," came the reply. "I'll do the decorating round here; we can't afford someone else to do it. I'll paint and change the wallpaper, you can clear up afterwards."

Well, that is very much to the point. I have never done anything like it before. At home, the landlord came, looked round and decided which rooms needed redecorating. At regular intervals, as far as I remember, every three years, such a visit occurred. If there was anything wrong with the gas, electricity or water, my father would ring him. He himself could hardly put a picture up without help. Somebody came for everything: putting the long velvet curtains up, changing light fittings, checking the central heating system. I had known since childhood that if you were not a manual worker you would not touch these things. Status!

Now there will be a whole house to look after. Yes, and that garden. And washing for three people. I have to learn to cook the English way, too. Roy is not very happy with German dishes, such as cabbage, potato soup, German type sausages. Would I have help in the house as I had known way back in the past? The answer is a definite 'no', but with a smile: "Roy and I will help you, You'll see."

19 November 1947

"I'd like to go and see something of Princess Elizabeth's wedding," I said to Dick. We were in the kitchen doing the washing up and listening to the BBC reporting on the crowds gathering round the Palace and Westminster.

"What?" Dick was appalled. "We would have to take the first underground train from Newbury Park. I don't even know when. Perhaps 6 o'clock in the morning? No way, my love, you are on your own."

"Ah well, will you wake me?" His rejection of my idea was absolutely all I needed. I was determined.

"You really mean it, don't you?" He sounded confused.

"Yes, I do. This is something that is fast disappearing in our world. I'd like to see the procession, sense the strength of tradition in this country, feel I belong to all the crowds in the West End. Don't you see? Besides, Philip has German blood." I winked at my husband: "There are special ties between him and myself."

"What a speech! Sorry, darling, you get carried away. I don't. Count me out. But I'll wake you. When?"

Late evening *20 November 1947*

At five o'clock this morning I had to walk to the station, as there were no buses at that time. It was a grey, wet November morning. I was not at all sure I made the right decision. Newbury Park and overcrowded platforms! I had not made a mistake! Hundreds of people waiting for the first train into town. Where would I have to change? Oxford Circus for Westminster perhaps? I listened. Yes, lots of passengers seemed to do that. So I joined them.

I made my way to Parliament Square. No, I did not make my way; I was swept along in an enormous crowd moving in one direction, singing, shouting, passing round thermos flasks and bottles of every kind, carrying children on their shoulders. I was one of them, couldn't get away even if I wanted to. I felt very, very good, despite the cold and wet. Hours went by before great events took place. When they did, I was well rewarded: a glimpse of Winston Churchill, complete with cigar, nodding and smiling, all the members of the Royal Family and, in a coach out of Grimm's fairytales, Princess Elizabeth and Prince Philip.

Maybe I am a stupid romantic, but where in the world today can you see such an unbroken line of royal tradition, pomp and circumstance, as Elgar called it, and the manifestation of love and joy, of hope for the world?

How different from Hitler demonstrations! Here is absolute spontaneity.

25 November 1947

I begin enjoying the role of a proper housewife. Bread and milk deliveries, the laundryman calls, they are absolutely new experiences. The chimney-sweep was a bit of a nightmare because of the havoc he created in the living rooms. The window cleaner will come once a month not only to do his work, but to stop and chat in the kitchen over a cup of tea.

Visits to new friends make me realise how universal it is to invite a neighbour – or a tradesman – to have a cup of tea, practically any time of the day. An English custom I want to adopt. German invitations for an afternoon coffee, admittedly with a mouth-watering selection of pastries, had been rather strenuous. You had to take flowers and, quite frequently, dress for the occasion.

That nice cup of tea, the elixir of life, panacea. Whenever we are invited to stay in any of our relatives' homes, we have a cup of tea early in the morning (to wake us), then it is tea for breakfast and again, at mid-morning. After lunch as well and of course tea, at tea time late in the afternoon. And, if we like it, quite often before going to bed. Oh for a good, strong cup of coffee. Not that I dislike tea. In fact, it can be far more refreshing than coffee. In Germany, the Frisians are the biggest tea drinkers. Along the East coast of Schleswig-Holstein and on the islands there, the average tea consumption per person per day is fifteen cups! With milk or without, with lemon and, in winter, definitely with rum.

It reminds me of an incident when I was a student in London. I realised then how bad my English was. At an afternoon tea party, the hostess went round refilling cups. She came to me and I said 'thank you'. She promptly gave me more tea. I obediently drank it, although I did not want it. After a while, she did the rounds again.

"Would you like another cup?"

"Thank you," I replied, and she lowered the pot.

"No" – I in an urgent voice – "I don't want any more."

"Oh?"

"I am sorry, I mean, no thank you."

An embarrassed silence everywhere.

"What I mean is, in Germany we say 'please' if we want more and 'thank you' if we don't."

Laughter all round. I was able to translate English literature, but could not cope with little idiosyncrasies like these.

26 November 1947

Roy is going to the local Junior School and has found friends in the neighbourhood. Occasionally he has to defend his new Mum and we are such good friends now that he really stands up for me.

"Can I have a boy here for tea?" he asked one

afternoon, coming home from school.

"Yes, of course you can, darling. One or more? Who is it?"

I held my breath. I sounded exactly like my mother who had always carefully scrutinised the children – or rather, the children's parents – I wanted to invite. I do not want to sound like that, ever.

"I mean, when do you want him to come?"

"Just one boy." All of a sudden he sounded embarrassed. "He is always teasing me about you. He says you speak funny and, if you are German, you'll beat me one day."

"I see. And you want to prove to him that I don't?"

"Well, I *know* you don't and you won't. He is *terribly* stupid, and I want him to find out. But he is really very nice."

Obviously, I was a little taken aback, to be looked over by an eight year old and have it decided by him if I am a child beater.

I put my arms round Roy. "It's alright, darling, we'll show him. You know, I love you?"

He still does not say 'Mummy' to me. How I long in such moments to hold Henning close to me.

"Oh yes, and I love you nearly as much as Daddy. I mean ..."

"I know what you mean, no more, hm? What is it to be? Crumpets, (which he loves), cup cakes, jelly? You tell me."

"Beans on toast and ice-cream," he decided in a very firm voice.

"Right. You just let me know when he wants to come."

The war has not yet been forgotten, and young boys are still fighting the Jerries although many parents I come to know are not. Sometimes the comment is:

"We don't think much of your people after all you've done to the world, but *you* seem to be alright." What more can I ask for?

Venturing into a butcher's the other day – not my own butcher, the old soldier, with whom I have long Anglo-German conversations – he asked me, wrapping the mutton I bought, the by now familiar question: "Where are you from? Sweden?"

I have far more courage now and answered: "Why? I am English."

"You are?" His eyes widened. "But where from? You don't quite sound it."

I laughed. "I am German born, but I have an English husband, and an English passport."

"Ah, then you are British," and he smiled.

What a subtle difference and yet, what a valid one!

A letter arrived from the PTA of Roy's school. Thank goodness, the letter head told me what PTA means. I had no idea. It asked if we would be willing to help at the school bazaar in two weeks time.

"I've been wondering about this and wanted to enquire. What do you think?" Dick asked.

"I don't know. I don't understand. This is a school affair. Why don't the staff take care of it?"

"There are lots of practical ways in which parents can help school finances and, anyway, many parents like to be involved." Dick was very patient, as usual.

"Yes, alright. So, the bazaar is supposed to bring in money for the school. Why? Everything is free: books, paper – I am a little confused."

"I know," he answered, "but think of school excursions, for instance, and special educational outings which not all parents can afford. Think of the exchange of school uniforms or of sports days. There are so many areas where help is needed, even giving the odd classroom a fresh coat of paint."

We used to have parents' evenings when I was at school, they were formal sessions with an address by the headmistress. My mother, who always attended them, was never impressed, she used to call them a 'waste of time'. I asked Dick about such meetings.

"Oh no," he laughed, "here you get complaints, lively discussions on many problems concerning the children and, if you belong to the PTA, you really get to know the teachers. That is a very important point."

It sounded good and useful to me. Dick says I can probably help with the washing up to start with. But he has grand plans for himself: to run a stall. When we told Roy about our involvement he was very pleased with his parents.

2 December 1947

Dick has revived a few friendships and discovered that one of his oldest friends has moved into our neighbourhood, together with his wife and two children. I like Joyce. She helps me a great deal getting to know the art of shopping. Supermarkets are only just beginning to put in an appearance, and it is very important to know your grocer and butcher, particularly, as a number of vital supplies are still rationed. I am lucky. They seem to accept me, chat about the war in a lighthearted way that does not hurt me at all, drop the odd German phrase they have picked up. I am doing quite well. I soon learn the sort of bacon to buy, which cuts of meat to ask for (I have never known bacon for breakfast, and meat in Germany is cut in a very different way), what to put into a meat pie and what haggis really is. Joyce's family came from Scotland.

I have learned how to make a Christmas Pudding. Or I thought I had. When I produced it last night, so that I could get the family's verdict, it was far too light and Dick called it 'quite a nice College Pudding'. They laughed and I joined in, but I shall never make a Christmas Pudding again. I argue with myself: a person can have many roles and yet none to perfection. I think that is a very convincing defence on my part.

3 December 1947

Today I had my first real shock. Joyce and I were out together when Joyce suggested we should go and see her mother. As I had time, I accepted her invitation.

When the door opened, a statuesque, rather stern looking lady greeted her daughter with 'come in', looked at me, and when Joyce said, "Mother, this is Pat; I told you about her," she drew back.

"Hello, Mrs Hammond," I said. "Joyce talked to me about you and your family."

"And did she tell you about her brothers? They never came back from the war."

"Yes, I know. All I can say is, I think I can feel your sorrow and understand it."

"Well, then you'll understand too that I don't want you in my house. It is not you, it is simply anything German. I can't, I can't. Give me time."

And she left the hall abruptly. I was still standing there; Joyced looked very embarrassed. I left after a few words with poor Joyce.

Walking back to our house on my own I was no longer as calm as I may have appeared to Joyce. This was the only time so far of absolute refusal to be accepted, without even trying to find out what I am really like. It hurt me deeply and I realised how vulnerable I am. What is more, this has happened so soon after we have settled in our own home and I am beginning to grow roots. It is a rebuff I shall long remember.

At the same time, I can well imagine how a German mother would have reacted in similar circumstances. She might not even have shown the same restraint, so characteristic of the British. They are so reticent about the passionate display of joy and sorrow, quite unlike the Germans.

6 December 1947

Christmas, my first English Christmas, is less than three weeks away. I have prepared a parcel to send to my parents and to Henning, who presents no problem: a football, sketch pads and crayons – he loves drawing – a mouth organ, biscuits and sweets. He will be very pleased. For my family in Kiel, however, it is going to be the strangest collection of presents I have ever sent to anyone: sewing needles, cotton, knitting wool and needles, shoelaces, elastic, stockings, warm scarves and gloves and, of course, cocoa, tea and coffee, as much as I am allowed to. They are all goods which are unobtainable in Germany at present and – to my mind – plentiful here, although some of them are rationed. There is a very strict customs control in both countries. Supplies in England are limited and it is not good policy to support the raging black market in Germany.

And this first Christmas in England I want to start

something I intend to continue all my life. This is important to me – celebrating Christmas Eve as people in Germany do – decorating the tree with live candles, keeping the tree a secret from the children until the evening (if possible, lock the door) and then, when everything is ready and the candles lit, calling the children in with a little bell. A carol first, and afterwards they can look for their presents under the tree. In the end, a festive supper. I do not at all like Christmas trees with electric lights, seen in the windows of houses long before Christmas.

We explained all this to Roy and mentioned that, like good children everywhere, he would probably find a Christmas stocking filled with goodies in the morning. He and Dick think this is marvellous: Roy, because it would make his Christmas longer than that of other children, and Dick because he would not have to get up at dawn on Christmas morning.

Christmas Eve, 1947

But oh, the best laid plans! Long after dark, we were still alone: my mother-in-law, Roy and I. Dick had not returned from an office party he had talked about in the morning.

"Sometimes they go on a bit," Grandma said. "Perhaps you should not have done this, anyway," she continued. "Good old English Christmas as it is should be sufficient, don't you think?"

"Maybe," I replied. "But I thought Dick would like it as well. And, please try to understand, it is the one and only tradition that is important to me. Because I think it is very beautiful, I hoped it would be a pleasure to all of us."

"Of course," she smiled. "That was a silly remark I made. Please forget it. I'm sure Dick won't be very long, and then we can celebrate."

We played yet another game of Ludo. And then I became angry. Last year I was alone at Christmas – Dick was in England – at a time when I was going through a very unhappy period. This year it was going to be beautiful, even without him. I left Roy and Grandma in the dining room, lit the candles on the tree and called them with a small brass bell we have.

Roy, speechless, dived for the presents. But I stopped him. First a Carol. So we sang *Silent Night* a little tentatively on my part. I am still not very sure of the English translation of that old German carol. It has to be better next year.

There was a big fire in the hearth and the tree glittered with lametta and colourful decorations. The whole room was filled with the warm glow of Christmas.

I felt I had to be very firm with myself. This Christmas was going to be good, Dick or no Dick. I could not spoil it by showing my disappointment. Taking a deep breath, I went to fetch drinks, nuts and some chocolates and nearly dropped the tray when I returned. Roy was jumping up, trying to hug me and shouting: "Thank you, Mummy, thank you!"

"For this?" I asked, pointing to the tray.

"No, everything. All this, and the tree tonight."

I smiled. He had called me 'Mummy'. This was my Christmas present from him. I felt richly rewarded.

And then my husband came in.

"I am sorry. Gosh, I really am very sorry. I forgot."

And he promptly fell asleep in an armchair. It was funny, and the mounting eruption of anger subsided within me. This evening could not be as important to him as it is to me. But he will have to learn; this is never going to happen again.

5 January 1948

Open fires in lounges and dining rooms, in old inns as well, are every German's idea of British life style. Certainly very beautiful and cosy, I think, as I watched Dick lighting a fire one evening, even if one feels a dreadful draught from the back while sitting in front of it. With one or two exceptions, at the end of the war, when I tried to cook something in the open, I have hardly ever lit a fire, and that had been with dry twigs. There seems to be a different technique here to get coal burning. Not easy. I must learn this. It will be so nice for

Roy and Dick to come home to a blazing fire, not just to electric heaters.

So I've tried it today. Dick's mother arrived to spend the weekend with us. Paper, wood, coal were at the ready. The wood was alight but, as soon as I put the coal on it, I effectively extinguished all signs of life. I had seen Dick using a newspaper, blocking off the hearth and thereby creating a draught under the fire. I tried that. Flames appeared burning the newspaper. I was flat on my stomach by then, blowing into the flickering flame, as Dick's mother walked in. The kitchen door is always open.

"What are you doing down there?" Was the first thing she said.

I was very annoyed with myself. "I did so want to have a fire going before you came. I'm no good at all with this."

"Try sugar," she said in a dry voice. "It will burn beautifully."

"How much? Sugar is rationed."

"Oh, you don't need much. Besides, you can have my share. I only need very little."

I went to the kitchen and came back with a one-pound bag of sugar.

"No, no," she cried, "you just sprinkle a little on top of the fire."

It worked like a dream. Both Roy and Dick were

delighted when they came home, although Dick worried about his mother: "You shouldn't. You don't do that type of work in your house now, because you must not bend low. And you know it."

"What do you mean," she answered. "I didn't. Pat lit it."

She never said anything about the sugar, and I felt very grand.

People certainly live with fires and seem to understand them much better than I do. One evening, standing at our bedroom window, I saw sparks flying. They came from a chimney diagonally across the road. I did not know the people but, as a good neighbour, felt it my duty to warn them. I went across and rang the bell. When I informed the lady about the fire all she had to say was: "Isn't it a nuisance? I put water on the fire. It's out now. Never mind, it'll have to wait until my husband comes home."

Fire, fire on the roof! A picture of the past flashes through my mind. This little woman does not know anything about it. Perhaps she had never been in an air-raid, had never been forced to leave everything she owned and a home that might collapse any moment under a roof on fire. To her it was just 'a nuisance', something her husband would see to. To me it brought back the horror of a night when the roof of our block of flats was ablaze, and my sister and I tried to extinguish some of the flames, tried to make the old people in the house abandon their rooms. No husbands or young men were there to help us.

Will I ever really understand these people? Outwardly so calm which does not mean that they are not disturbed. It is simply deeply ingrained in their nature not to make a fuss. There is a casual acceptance of problems which, in my old country, would result in something akin to panic.

In conversation with Dick's family I learn something of the behaviour of English people under air-raid conditions. How they had parties and sing-songs in the communal air-raid shelters, sometimes even with a piano underground. Perhaps to shut out the fear? How this contrasted with my nights in German shelters! No cups of tea or coffee, hardly any talk, only the whimpering of children from time to time. No talk, because we did not want to show fear and through that fear perhaps express doubts or feelings that could be construed as treacherous. There was always a Nazi warden of some authority nearby.

Both of us find it most enjoyable to spend an evening by the fireside, listening to 'ITMA' or 'Much Binding in the Marsh', neither of which I understand fully yet, or reading to each other. And sometimes, with a drink in hand, just talking.

"Contented?" Dick asked, and we burst out laughing. It reminds us of the one and only occasion when Klaus, my first husband, and Dick had met. I then worked as an interpreter for Dick. We had left the office together and Klaus was waiting for me outside. I introduced them, and Klaus said in his slightly stilted, very careful English: "How do you do? Are you content with my wife?"

I felt very embarrassed. He had meant 'satisfied with her work'. I realised this at once. Dick, however, did not know that there is only one word in German to describe 'content' and 'satisfied'. He looked utterly bewildered. I was only working for him at that time.

8 January 1948

Somebody at work told Dick there is a German Brides Club in Romford. We decided to go to one of their meetings. I was not at all sure, but curious. We set off to a Church Hall in Romford, a friendly place, brightly painted, a little coffee bar in one corner. Coffee, not tea. There they meet, with or without their husbands, once a month. There were about fifteen of them, nearly all considerably younger than I. They are the eighteen, nineteen years old girls who married British Soldiers. In Germany life with them had been fun, but once they came to England and the men left the Forces, there was often a bleak future ahead: no home for the young couple, no job in the beginning, and the hard task for the young girls to learn the language. Not one of those I talked to that evening spoke reasonable English. They had never learnt it at school but, quite naturally, quickly picked up the rough language of the soldiers. I had never heard 'bloody' being used so often in such a short time. Most of them still lived with the husband's family which created various problems. How fortunate I have been: I found myself nodding agreement when they poured out their complaints, if only to please them.

"You must know too how it is," they said.

"Yes, of course, but you get used to their ways. Are you trying to cook English dishes? Won't you go to Evening Classes?" I was desperately searching for something encouraging to say. They all looked at me. Silence.

"I'm going home for the whole of summer," one of them suddenly burst out, "I can't take the life here."

"That won't help. We all have to work very hard at our marriages. You love your husband?" I took her arm.

"Yes, but I didn't think it would be like this. I can't even ask you in for a cup of coffee. My mother-in-law wouldn't like it."

This underlined the resentment some of them must have met in their husband's family. It all seems so different from my experience. Is it perhaps because they do not offer enough to be accepted? Dick and I looked at each other. I felt guilty. I immediately suppressed an impulse to invite her to our house. No, this is not what I want for us, we have overcome many of the initial problems mainly because we started life together with our eyes wide open, wary of pitfalls. We are older as well. I think that half of these young girls will, within a short period, try to return to Germany, they will give up. This is not the promised land they had expected. And if they are not allowed to go back for good, holding a British Passport? There is no chance at present of dual nationality. Some of them will, no doubt, go under in a big city.

We shall never go the German Brides Club again.

1 February 1948

One of the radio programmes we both like very much is the Sunday record request show 'Two Way Family Favourites', linking BAOR, the British Army of Occupation of the Rhine, with their families and friends at home. Over there are the soldiers, no longer fighting but occupying enemy country and, in their own way, enjoying the outcome of the war. They make contact with Germans. Perhaps they will begin to like some of them, to understand them? And here are their families, longing for them to come home. A bridge is being built. Would it not be wonderful if I could reach my family in this way, if I could say 'hello' to Henning? What a silly thought! I have to dismiss it at once. Still, maybe one day . . .

'Family Favourites' are for many people a regular accompaniment to Sunday lunch. For us as well. And, if we do not go out, Richard Dimbleby takes us and millions of others 'Down Your Way', all over Britain. I love that programme, a weekly portrait of a village or town through the voices of its inhabitants. Not only can I listen to people from the Hebrides to London, from Edinburgh to Cornwall, but I can also enjoy the absolute mastery of Dimbleby's craft as an interviewer. He seems close to everyone. His interest in ordinary lives makes me feel as if we are all important to him.

For an evening's listening there is, once a week, 'Twenty Questions', again with Richard Dimbleby. Half the nation is wondering week after week if a problem in the programme is animal, vegetable or mineral.

In Germany, after years of military music, propaganda speeches and endless reports of the news on various battlefields, the occupying forces are now controlling the radio stations. That applies to newspapers as well. *Die Welt* (The World), the first paper licensed in the British Zone, contains very little important material other than that translated from the English press. The national press here and illustrated magazines like the *Picture Post* are a never ending source of interest to me. I gradually begin to comprehend what 'freedom of the press' actually means.

From where we live, it is very easy for me to take a fast Green Line bus or the Underground train to conquer London. I have time now. The household is running smoothly, Roy is at school. I feel a great sense of adventure visiting the National Gallery or any art exhibition I find advertised in the papers, strolling through the City, spending hours in Foyles' (which to me is not a bookshop, but an enormous international library), or just sitting on the steps of Eros in Piccadilly Circus listening to passers-by. And I have to listen hard to distinguish any English around me. The whole world seems to meet at the graceful little statue. Bayswater and Hendon attract me too. Many German Jews have settled there. It is a place where one hears more German than English, where the delicatessen shops smell of my home country and remind me of the past. There are times, though not often, when I need that, when I have to argue with myself that I am not on a visit, not a tourist. I have no return ticket. I want to live and work here. London is warm and friendly, but I am still very much an outsider. I have to conquer that. In a gathering with Dick's colleagues I heard somebody say: "She is not English. Her English is too good." It reminds me of Shaw's 'Pygmalion', where someone remarks about Eliza: 'She must be foreign. No English person can speak English so perfectly.'

What it really amounts to is this: I would be better if I were not so good.Funny, but correct. I speak text book English. Who knows? In time it could become blurred at the edges and I may even acquire a local accent. The main problem at the moment seems to be my selective choice of expressions and failure to use the everyday little ones. Take 'to get', for example. The amazing number of meanings that tiny word can convey! When studying English I was always told not to 'avail myself' too much of it. It was not considered to be good English. Well, everybody else uses it and, if it helps to be accepted on level terms, I shall do it as well.

In our French lessons at school I learned: 'Tout le monde a deux patries, la sienne et la France.' (Everyone has two motherlands: his own and France). In my case, this has *got* to be changed to 'his own and England'.

13 February 1948

I asked Dick if he would like to go shopping with me this weekend. There is still a feeling of apprehension in me when it comes to big purchases, such as meat for the weekend, and I like him to make the decisions. He, on the other hand, loves to give his time to Roy on Saturday, playing games with him when the weather is bad, or going into the country with us when the sun is shining.

"Alright, let's all three go," and, slightly threatening, "provided it does not take the whole afternoon."

I promised him it would not.

Ilford High Street was full of shoppers. Dick held Roy's hand and I walked on the outside.

"Let's change over," he suddenly said and moved me away from the curb.

"Why," I asked. "A lady always walks on the right."

"She does not, not in my country. Didn't you know?"

He is often teasing me with 'his' country.

"Know what? It is one of the first courtesies a young man learns in Germany: Lady on the right."

"Then we are more courteous than Germans. The gentleman walks on the outside, near the curb. That may be left or right. This has been so ever since ladies had to be protected from being splashed by horses or carriages."

"I was thinking about this when Roy suddenly started: "I know, Daddy, and when a bus or car comes, you'll be run over and not Mummy."

"That's right, son," Dick laughed, "and one day you'll have that privilege."

Whatever else is there I have to learn in this new country of mine?

After walking in the Park — *7 March 1948*

Gradually I become restless. We are very happy, but the one thing missing is another child. I hear Roy's incessant chatter, and when I close my eyes for a moment, I hear a different voice, equally bright, full of fun. Henning is so far away and there is no possibility of seeing him yet. I yearn for an English baby. So does Dick. One more child in the family might help to still the pain, forever present.

The past closes quickly behind young children. Roy no

longer seems to miss his mother, Henning's letters and drawings for me make me think he is happy as well. There is, nevertheless, always the gnawing longing for him. I have to do something to fill that void. A job perhaps? Eventually we would need extra money to visit Henning or to pay for him to come and see us, and I feel it is really my task to provide for that, although at present the chance of travelling to Germany as a civilian does not exist.

27 March 1948

Yes, a job is the answer. I have replied to several advertisements by City firms asking for secretaries with knowledge of French, occasionally also of German. Trade with Germany is practically non-existent; Swiss and Austrian companies, however, are sometimes interested. I have attended a few interviews. People are friendly, but the answer is always the same: "It is too early to bring a German into our firm. Our staff lost fathers, brothers . . . You understand, we cannot afford to – perhaps – create an atmosphere. We think you should wait another year. Please, nothing against you personally." I understand. It is something I simply have not thought about, because everybody has been so friendly, generally.

But I really do want to work. Factories employ many DP's, displaced persons. Why not a German on a shop floor?

29th March 1948

Today I went to the Plessey Company, where Dick works, but I did not tell him. No problem. I could start work at once, I was told, in a big assembly hall. I have been given a job which is new to the Company, and my instructions were given to me by an engineer from the Development Department. The assembly consists of two tiny components of dissimilar metals and a small pellet of braising material. The three components have to be put together in a small jig and fed into a special oven. The parts are so tiny and my fingers so clumsy, I feel I am doing the job with boxing gloves on! The engineer waffled on about controlled atmosphere, furnaces and other technicalities which I would never have understood in German, let alone in English. In spite of this I managed to produce acceptable work, often with the aid of my co-workers in the hall, although I have not discovered what those parts are for.

We are all women in that big assembly hall, most of us not British, but there is a great feeling of togetherness. All work part time, most have families, but some of them are still separated through the war. There are Poles, Estonians, French, and there are Polish, Baltic and French songs while we work. There is a lot of laughter and interesting conversation while we eat our sandwiches at lunchtime. I know I shall be very proud of myself when I take home my first weekly pay of three Pounds ten Shillings.

But I shall wait for the right moment to tell Dick. He

will be surprised, and pleased, I think.

23 April 1948

Well, he is not. Today disaster struck. Dick walked through the big hall with some visitors, showing them something at the far end of the room. And he spotted me. I have hardly ever seen him really angry, but he was when he came home. Hurt pride that his wife works in a factory? Embarrassment? Or simply upset because I had not told him?

"If you are so set on work you might as well do something you understand," he said when he arrived.

After his visit, I was called to the Personnel Director and, at the same time, had to face the Export Sales Manager who is looking for a secretary.

"Why didn't Dick tell us you were looking for a job? We met at the firm's Christmas dinner, don't you remember?"

He seemed vaguely familiar. There have been so many new faces. A very pleasant man.

"Can you type? Are you well organised? Occasionally there is French correspondence. Do you think you could cope?"

"I hate shorthand," I replied. I am silly, I know. But I do not want a job this way. I want to find it alone.

"There needn't be shorthand," he said quickly.

"But I can do it."

"Fine. Get rid of your overalls and tell the foreman that you are going over to Sales. I'd like to see you later in my office."

I felt so guilty when I told the women in the 'shop'. "Good for you," they said, "what a thing to have brain as well as beauty. Come and see us once in a while." Which I shall do.

30 April 1948

Suddenly I have a good, interesting type of work, with considerably more money than before. And I know – as I do quite often – Dick was right. But I still go down to the shop floor to eat my sandwiches with the wonderful women I had met. I love listening to their songs. And their 'Hello, Pat' is always cheerful and welcoming.

19 June 1948

This was only the beginning. I did not stay long with the Plessey Company. As usual, I think about what I would really like to do: teach German. It is, however, not exactly the favourite subject in schools; in fact, hardly any curriculum includes it. So, industry or commerce it has to be. The fact that I have had a position opens doors in the City. Perhaps it is just that nobody wants to be the first to employ a German.

Last week, I started with a somewhat strange secretarial post in a tiny office, a one-man set-up from which thousands of pounds worth of raw rubber are pushed around the world, a continual cycle of buying and selling, all done over the telephone. The director had been a victim of anti-semitic politics in Austria and had emigrated to England before the outbreak of the Second World War. He speaks good French but has never really mastered the English language, with the result that all English calls have to be taken and answered by me, with him hovering by my side, whispering: "Vat does he vant?" and "tell him to vait." The call finished, he pulls a duster, smelling of disinfectant, out of his desk drawer and wipes the telephone vigorously. It never occurs to him that this is rather hurtful and humiliating for me. Strange, because he is a very kind and considerate employer. He, however, never says 'Hello, Pat' when I arrive. It is always: "Good morning, Mrs Skinner, how are you?" I feel sure it has a lot to do with his upbringing.

10 July 1948

We have to think about Roy's summer holidays. They present a problem, as I can only be away from work for one week. We have to plan this very carefully, perhaps, one week for Roy and me alone, two weeks for Roy on Uncle Ken's farm and two weeks for father and son.

That should cover it. But what about Dick and me? It's not very satisfactory and I feel a little disgruntled.

"We'll have many years ahead when things will work out better. It is a shame you've only recently started your job," Dick said.

"Do you think Roy and I could go to Walton? I'd love to be with Auntie Rose." Suddenly I felt much brighter. "I'll ring her."

"Yes, and then Roy and I go camping for one week, perhaps in the New Forest. He'd like that. And the next week we'll be at home looking after you when you come back, after a long day's work." This with a slightly mocking smile.

Perhaps it will work out better than I imagine now.

3 August 1948

Roy and I had a beautiful week in dear Walton. Every day was a glorious summer day. Very early in the morning we walked along the beach. We bought a newspaper, sometimes a comic, and on the way back collected a big bag full of hot, oven-fresh rolls from Mr. Wright, the local baker. Then into the big kitchen, where some member of the family was already grilling sausages and bacon and frying mushrooms which had been gathered that morning from the meadows nearby.

Big pots of tea and coffee were waiting for us. After

breakfast, back to the beach or up to the steep cliffs of the Naze for kite flying, once or twice taking a small boat on the backwaters, or simply a lazy day in a deckchair, contemplating a swim, but not always going into the water which is exceptionally cold this summer.

Roy and I were very happy that week and very close. I am so grateful.

Kensington Gardens *5 September 1948*

This is the last holiday weekend for Roy, and he and Dick have gone to the Science Museum. I am sitting by the Round Pond, in the sun. Not that I dislike the Science Museum, but Dick's never ending enthusiasm for machinery of all kinds does not create the same feeling in me. I have been there several times. Enough is enough. Let father and son enjoy it together.

We are pleased with the way the holidays went. It was

very nice being alone with Dick, when Roy was on the farm. No baby sitters needed! And yet, better still was last week when my two men looked after me when I arrived home from the office. No cooking or washing-up, no laundry or vacuum-cleaning – I felt very spoilt.

From Monday on it will be back to normal.

15 November 1948

Dick rang me at work this afternoon saying that the fog was very thick around Ilford. He had just listened to the weather report – it was going to get bad everywhere. He said I should ask Mr 'What's-his-name' (it is an unpronouncable name for Dick) if I could leave then. I was a bit surprised as it was only one o'clock.

Dick sounded very definite, though. I did not know what all the fuss was about. A bit of fog, I thought. But I obeyed him. And when I told my boss that I had to be at Newbury Park Station by two o'clock he actually encouraged me to hurry up and go. He seemed concerned too. No doubt he knew more about it than I did.

I stepped out of the station and stopped dead. I tried to look around – nothing. A thick grey blanket. I couldn't believe it!

"Hello, Pat." What a relief! Dick took my hand.

"Where is Roy? How will he get home?" Seeing the

fog, I became very concerned. "It's all been taken care of. I rang Mrs. Andrews. She'll pick up her Martin and Roy."

I couldn't see at all, and Dick certainly had not been exaggerating on the telephone.I would never have found my way on my own. I heard voices, but every sound was muffled, as it is very often in Germany in thick snow. And I still couldn't see, not even a hand in front of my face. Even in the darkest, unlit nights during the war I have not experienced such a complete obliteration of all normal features. I did not want to breathe. I had to, of course, but there was a dank, smoky smell in the air, spread by endlessly swirling grey masses of fog. I was very frightened and gripped Dick's arm.

He led me with the instinct of a blind man. The voices again: Questions like 'are we on the Southend Road?' and 'how far to Whalebone Lane?'

We knew we had about two miles to go. We bumped into other people going in the same direction. We linked up. One long chain of lost children! An eerie atmosphere, so very quiet, with the central reservation of the dual carriage way lit up by flares, put there by the police, occasionally spotlighting the buses and cars pulled up by the side of the road, out of action. I felt very tired, walking became strenuous, my coat felt sodden, I kept on wiping my eyes.

At last, home. We opened the front door, switched on the light and froze. Not only I, Dick as well. Fog had penetrated through the key holes – grey mist was swirling under the lamp in the hall. I looked into the long mirror facing me, took my scarf off and could hardly recognise myself. Streaks of black soot were running down my face. Bits of hair not covered by the scarf showed dark grey and wet.

"Wait till I tell my folks about a thing like this," I laughed, "nobody will believe me."

"Well, then they'll have to come here in winter."

It does not happen every year, so they tell me. That's what a combination of fumes, smoke and fog can do. It is horrible. What a health hazard it is, too.

I think of clear, sunny winter days, especially in North Germany, with blue skies,when the air is dry and the temperature well below zero, the snow crunching under my feet, and when it is a pleasure to walk along a frozen river or watch children and adults skating on a pond. A picture in my mind which Breughel might have painted.

30 November 1948

I could not bear working for my raw rubber man any longer. There is a great need in me to be with English people, not to be cut off, with only the presence of one 'foreigner', even if he is a very pleasant person. I've started studying newspaper adverts once more.

A translator is needed for a large chemical firm in Stratford East. I've applied for the post and have gone for an interview.

They have a number of German chemical processes there, for dyes mainly. They were confiscated at the end of the war and have to be translated. Would I be able to do that, I was asked.

"I don't know much about chemistry but, given a good technical dictionary, I think I could."

"I feel sure you can cope," a very pleasant young research chemist looked at me through thick lenses and smiled. "We had to have references from your previous employer, and they are very good. I'm sorry, but references are necessary in your case, you understand?"

Yes, I understand. This is a very English firm, a well-established family concern. I am probably the only foreigner amongst several hundred people.

He led me to a small office which was to be my working place.

"I hope you'll like it here. You need a quiet place to work."

When I started, a few days ago. I found everything I needed, a good typewriter, a number of dictionaries and a whole pile of slightly old looking files.

But oh! it is a lonely job. The only thing to do to offset that isolated feeling is to explore the neighbourhood in my lunch hour: the smell of the fish meal factory nearby, the canal with the odd dead rat at the banks, cobbled back streets with mean little houses – my first encounter with slums. Not that they did not exist in Germany. Compensation is to be found in the local market with its fruit and vegetable stalls, stands with jellied eels, and a fishmonger trying to rescue and trap live eels in the gutter, after a crate has turned over. The smells are different. No whiff of lovely burnt almonds or hot potato pancakes, no organ grinders either – they seem to have disappeared everywhere – and no fishmonger or butcher wearing a clean white apron. Yes, cleanliness is lacking too, compared to German markets. Still, when I buy something, the chirpy humour of the cockneys, with rhyming slang sometimes, which I do not understand at all, reminds me of the humour and the quick, sharp response I have known in Berlin, amongst taxi drivers as well. They are tough, but not cynical, irrepressible, warmhearted men and women.

In the firm itself I only meet people if I go into the canteen. And then some of them are withdrawn, serious men absorbed in their work. Some play chess over lunch. However, two of them seek me out quite often with a very friendly 'Hello, Pat, will you eat with us?' They have a reason. They are eager to hear and learn about Germany and are ready to accept, at least in part, something which many Germans could still not come to terms with: their own recent history. They know Germany well and argue in a quiet, yet provocative way, perhaps waiting for my immediate counter attack. Germans, after all, have a reputation for loud and aggressive arguments, at least amongst themselves. This is different, constructive.

"Did you ever feel any hatred towards English people? I mean, during the war?"

The question is thrown at me one lunchtime. My fork stops midway between plate and mouth, then I put it down.

"No, I don't think so." I hesitate for a moment, and then very decidedly repeat. "No. Perhaps this is hard to explain," I continue, "but he went too far. Hitler, I mean."

"Like Kaiser Bill? He wanted supreme power before the first war."

I shake my head. "This was much worse. Ordinary people were not able to identify themselves with Hitler's ideas. They were afraid to speak up, yes, but they did not hate the British. Occupying all Europe! It was simply not realistic."

"You are right," one of them says. "It had to mean defeat."

"What are wars, anyway?" The other one quips. "Great big noisy games, and none of us really knows what about. Am I right?"

He is oversimplifying it, I think, but nod: "Yes, and on your side there was Churchill, a giant, a legendary figure to many Germans. How could I hate English people who had been challenged to face a war they did not ask for? How could I forget their kindness and easy friendliness when I was in London in 1936? No, I felt no hatred at all, only sadness that there had to be a deep gulf between two nations basically closer to each other than, for example, England and France."

"That was quite a speech, Pat. Thank you. And eat your chips, they are getting cold."

We laughed. I do enjoy their company.

The main question in all discussions with English people is for ever the same: Why had so few Germans raised their voices and tried to put a stop to all the horrific things done in the name of the nation? It is almost impossible for me to answer that question. They have never lived in the chains of a dictatorship and never known the fear of imprisonment and worse, for voicing an opinion against the government. I remember my first visit to Hyde Park, and told them about it.

"The English are bred in a country where protests have as much a place as fish and chips. They can say what they like. Listeners may laugh at you, take you seriously or turn away. But they can voice their opinion. I have been brought up to keep quiet, to accept whatever the authority demanded and to be a good obedient citizen. The difference, when I first discovered this freedom, shocked and overwhelmed me. Here I can speak out if I have anything to offer. What a beautiful thought!"

26 December 1948

This Christmas was a lot better. Dick did not forget about our party, and Roy enjoyed every bit of it, just like last year. But I miss Henning. He has written to me, although that is not the same. I long to be with him. How much longer will it be before I can see my boy, I wonder.

Thursday *10 March 1949*

Occasionally, I am wandering in a kind of no-man's-land. I have to try and inhibit strong emotional drives when I think of my German family and have to argue with myself that I do not have to like them just because we are related. The bonds of friendship can be so much stronger. Here I have somebody to come back to, always. I am never alone. If you do not have anybody, then you are really poor. My best friend is my husband. He understands my urge to work, he accepts the new people I have met and brought into the house, he even tolerates my 'thinking around the corner' as he calls it: the German side of me, probing the depths, considering all possibilities – too much and too often – and then rushing headlong into impulsive decisions, quite frequently the wrong ones.

I believe today the happiest couples are more like friends than anything else. Friendship takes precedence over passion. Yet the secret of being friends is not only that of closeness. You do not have to be obsessed with each other. Far from it. You can be busily engaged in a full life, part of which may well not be shared by your partner. But you know there is a loving person to whom you can turn in trouble.

There are certain events Dick does not want to share with me. He does not relish the thought of visiting Covent Garden or listening to a symphony concert, and I am never enthusiastic to wander around an engineering exhibition. We are, occasionally, glad to go our own way. So, when Auntie Rose rang and asked me if I would like to accompany her to the 'Ideal Home Exhibition', I was delighted. I had heard about it, but Dick declared that it would be very strenuous and crowded and – truly – quite boring. I did not argue. His attitude is only to go if you want to redesign your home. However, there is little money for that and we like our house as it is.

I met her in Liverpool Street Station, under the big clock at twelve o'clock.

I was thrilled. This 'aunt-in-law' does everything in style: a taxi from the Station, a beautiful lunch at Earls Court, close to the exhibition halls, and hours of wandering amongst stands showing a multitude of all the things one could possibly wish for in a home and garden. There had been the 'Gruene Woche' (green week) in Berlin before the war, although that concentrated on agriculture and gardens and was never as big as this.

Full of impressions, weary but very satisfied I returned home in the evening. What a lovely March day it was.

Spring in England. Daffodils and crocuses are out in the garden – much earlier than I had known in Germany – and it is time to welcome the warm season and put thick woollen winter clothes away for a few months. I decided to do that straight away.

"I wouldn't if I were you," Dick said.

"Why not? It's beautiful weather. What are you people always saying? Spring is in the air."

"Yes, but it can go again just as quickly," he warned.

"Nonsense, spring is spring," I argued. That was how it had been in my country. Once the snow started to melt in Stettin, towards the end of March, spring arrived suddenly with a burst of colour and that, after months of darkness, meant short white socks and bright dresses.

But I learnt it overnight. It does not mean that in England. Today, two days after I asked Dick to store a chest full of pullovers, scarves and woollen gloves in the loft, thick, rather wet snow covers the ground, and the garden has once more taken on a *wintry look*. How disappointing, Easter is only two weeks away.

"Never mind the weather," Dick said in a comforting voice, "it can change very quickly. We'll do something special this Easter – take a car. Can you drive?" he enquired.

I gasped. Funny, we have never talked about that before. I have been a little careful not to probe in this area. In Kiel he had the use of a car, and he loves driving. It would probably be far too expensive for us here. Money is his territory. He is generous where he can afford to be but, at the same time, a very good manager.

"Yes and no," I answered. "Klaus' uncle had a car, and I drove it sometimes. I'm sure I could not drive here, with so much traffic. And on the left side of the road, too."

I had a nasty experience riding Roy's bicycle in our road, which ended in a fall. For reasons I cannot define, riding on the left seems quite unnatural to me and creates great difficulties when it comes to turning into crossroads. However, if we had a car, it would be different. There would be four wheels this time.

"Are we going to have a car then?" I became excited.

"I've thought about it. Yes, we could. It would be nice, a run to the coast during weekends. We all love the sea. I could show you more of the country. Much easier than by bus or train. And later we could go to work together. You drop me off and then carry on to town."

I mentioned driving lessons and how expensive they are. But Dick just replied: "I'll give you lessons." How could he? He is not a qualified instructor. Dick soon pacified me explaining that all you have to be in order to teach someone to drive here is a 'non-disqualified' driver.

It is a relief to know that there is no written test here. I couldn't see myself answering questions on the theory of driving, especially in English.

30 March 1949

We have bought a little old Austin Cambridge for £50. It runs beautifully, but is in rather a deplorable state and we can see the road through the floorboards which, at times, can be quite frightening. Friends seem to think that this driving experiment could be a stumbling block in our easy-going relationship. It is not. I am perfectly happy to submit to my husband's instructions. I like arguing, but why should I in this case? Here is something he knows a lot more about than I do. And we work together, trusting each other. Most of the time, anyway. Now and again, however, I am reminded of friends' warnings that being taught by my husband would lead to short-tempered outbursts on either side, even to lingering resentment. I hope not.

3 April 1949

Well, they were right. Yesterday Dick and I were driving in the vicinity of our house, just a block away. It was quite late and very dark. This was the point of the exercise – I have very little experience in night driving. On our left was the entrance to a back road, serving a number of houses. Dick told me to drive past the entrance, then to stop and reverse into it. This I did, but oversteered, so that the rear of the car came into contact with a long wooden fence, made up of vertical weather boards. Our dear old car has spring steel bumpers, and the first sign that I had hit the fence was a loud click as the bumper travelled along the serrated surface. Dick's reaction was instant and very violent: "Stop!" My reaction was slow, mainly because of the indignation I felt about his tone of voice. There were a continuous succession of clicks before I came to a standstill.

"You stupid girl!" he growled, "come on, first gear forward."

I could not help giggling. Was it shock? Or simply that FGF (first gear forward) are the letters of the registration number of our car; FGF 357, which had not occurred to me before? I told him, but he did not laugh.

"When you are quite ready, Madam."

I pulled myself together and followed his instructions. Where the bumper had clicked going in one direction, it now dug in and tore off several boards before I was completely free of that fence. Dick was still furious:

"For heavens' sake, drive on. Nobody's seen us, and it is not a private fence. Let's get away from here."

"Do you think the bumper is damaged?" I asked.

"Never mind that. Just pull away. We are going home."

Nothing more was said until after I had parked the car, aiming it very carefully into our garage. Our neighbour left, having received a box of chocolates for looking after Roy, and we sat down. Dick exploded: "If I say 'stop', I mean it. There is no time for niceties, for saying 'please' or 'darling'. It simply means 'stop'. You have to accept that. Argue afterwards. Never mind the fence. That is council property. You are lucky."

I felt very small.

"Do you want to carry on teaching me? Or are you too angry?"

"Don't be silly,of course I'll go on. But for once, you'll have to obey immediately."

He sounded friendlier.

"I understand," I answered. "Still friends?"

"Well," he said in his slow way, "what about a Scotch to make peace?"

8 May 1949

The war finished exactly four years ago.

But what is more important is that at last now my dream will come true. We will be going to Germany soon, and I will be able to see Henning. He will be on holiday for Whitsun, and will come to Kiel to stay with Marianne and my parents.

It has been nearly two years since I last saw him. How will he react? He writes regularly, and we have been sending him presents that a ten-year-old boy in Germany these days longs for but still cannot get: football boots, fishing gear, even English comics. He is learning English at school now. It would be so funny to hear him speaking *my* adopted language!

How can I prove that I love him, and have longed to see him for the two years – nearly – that I have been here? I feel very apprehensive. I hope he can understand me.

16 May 1949

I passed!

How careful I have become during the last two weeks of learning to drive! I did not want to upset my husband again, I have never been as docile as in the past weeks, never paid as much attention to his instructions before, never smiled as gratefully when he rewarded me with a 'that was good'. It was not in vain, and I am absolutely thrilled: I have passed my driving test.

Those eight weeks of tension when driving in traffic,

of pure enjoyment on the open road, and of arguments with my instructor are over. I have a paper to say that I can drive. And, to prove it, I took Dick to his firm and intended to go shopping with Roy afterwards. As soon as his father left us Roy burst into tears and howled: "Can't we go by bus? I don't like you to drive alone."

It was a warm, sunny day, the car windows were open. At the traffic lights everybody seemed to look at me and guess that I am very new to the art of driving a car. I put on a haughty, defiant look. I'll show them!

What a feeling of power it gives me! The Western World is, on the whole, very male-orientated, and I am proud to have broken into men's reserve. There are many more women in England driving cars than there are in Germany. No doubt that will change. For the moment, however, I belong to those who say that driving a car and giving birth are the two greatest achievements in a woman's life.

Kiel *22 May 1949*
9 a.m.

We arrived at two a.m. last night and were welcomed by Gisela and Helmut at the station. They were the last Germans we saw before we left in 1947, and they were the first ones to greet us now. We are staying with them.

They look well. But the German Federal Republic

everyone talks about does not exist yet. Germany is still an occupied country and we need special travel permits and proof that we will be staying with relatives or friends. We also had to bring rations with us in the form of a large box filled with rice, sugar, flour, fat, cocoa, coffee and tea. They are *not* for the black market, but for our own consumption during our stay.

What a commotion! The box had to travel on its own and was subject to intense inspection at our arrival in Kiel.

I hardly slept last night. Very soon I will see Henning and my family. Will they welcome Dick? Have they mellowed towards me, their daughter and sister who, in my mother's words, 'left the sinking ship'? Their letters have always been superficial, non-commital. But I shall know the answer soon.

22 May 1949
9 p.m.

At last I saw Henning. I need not have worried about him at all. There was instant rapport. He was my son, I was his mother again as soon as we saw each other. He flew into my arms and then sat on my lap. That ten-year-old, lean, long-limbed boy whom I never wanted to be separated from.

He talked and talked endlessly – he has always been a big talker – about his friends, his father's school, and our holidays.

"Guess, what? I can stay for two whole weeks. Can you?"

That had been arranged earlier and was no news to me, but I fell in: "Really? Of course we can. We'll have a marvellous time."

But my parents, especially my mother, are as inflexible as ever. My father keeps quiet. When he talks to us, he sounds warm and friendly. He, now 68, has found a good position as an accountant in a building firm. Rebuilding the country, that is the foremost task, so there is plenty of work for everybody.

I sensed an air of sadness and resignation, though, in their little flat which Dick found for them two years ago. My heart went out to them.

"Can't you see I made the right decision for myself? I am happy. I can help you. Won't you let me?"

I meant practical help, naturally. That is all I can offer.

It is impossible to break through, just the same. There still lingers resentment that I got divorced and had left my son and my country. I cannot regain the closeness to Marianne either, that friendship which had seen us through the most difficult months of our lives.

My parents and my sister, are they envious? They comment on the clothes we wear, on our healthy looks, but when I said to Marianne, "You can have this jacket, please, I'll leave it here for you. Conditions generally are so much easier for us . . ." I recognised the same expression in her face she had shown me when we said goodbye in 1947: hard, the shutters down. None of them ever asks me if I am content, none wants to know if I am homesick sometimes or even, if I have ever thought of returning. And nobody says they would welcome me back. Although I know, of course, that such a question is, for the time being and under present political conditions, purely rhetorical.

I must come to terms with the fact that I seem to have lost my own family, but I shall not allow anything to overshadow this precious time with Henning.

Kiel *26 May 1949*

We've been playing on the beach, and having boat trips, football games for Henning and Dick and modest picnics. The only occasion when both Dick and I have to be very careful and not promise too much is when Henning repeatedly asks: "Can I stay with you? I can have a holiday in England soon, can't I?"

We know very well how strong the family resistance is in this case. Something we cannot bring ourselves to explain to him. We waive it by saying: "We must talk to your father about it. Besides, your English has to be good. Nobody will understand you. So, you must work hard at that."

Gisela and Helmut have not changed. In a way I am glad we cannot stay in my parents' small flat. There would be too much tension if we were with them all the time.

However, gradually Dick and I are getting desperate with our friends' hospitality. It is all about breakfast. Every morning Gisela dishes up eggs and bacon (she is incredibly good at discovering supplies where normally none exist), but there is also a mixed salad on the table.

"You people do like salad, don't you?" she asked on the first day.

"Yes, but" Dick started and I interrupted.

"What a lovely surprise. Yes, we do!"

Perhaps that was not too clever, because now there is a salad for breakfast on the table every morning. I do not have the heart to tell her that salad in the morning is just a little too much of a good thing, even if English people are fond of it at other mealtimes. I am so embarrassed!

It reminds me of the time after the war when we were invited by a German family to spend a weekend with them. They were butchers and, naturally, had everything to eat – not only meat – when the average German was hungry most of the time. Dick could not believe his eyes when for Sunday breakfast a huge gateau appeared on the table. A rich cake for breakfast? He confessed later that he had felt slightly ill at the sight of it. I loved it. I was not exactly used to it, but knew the custom from holidays in the country, particularly in South Germany, where it was served frequently.

Kiel – Friedrichsort *30 May 1949*

"You need some money," Gisela said today over breakfast.

"No. We brought food and we have our tickets. You know there is no exchange rate," was Dick's reply.

"Yes, but you want a little money in your pocket. Can't you sell something? One can buy a drink or a coffee now. Now and again even a meal." Gisela was always very practical.

"I have nothing to sell, I don't think so." Dick began to

wonder, I could tell.

"What about a suit? A pair of trousers? That would be very lucrative." She did not give up easily.

Dick laughed: "You wrote about a dance in the Yacht Club and knowing how formal you people can be, I brought my dinner jacket. Do I need it? It is somewhat tight anyway."

"Marvellous! No, you don't need it for that evening. Give it to me."

Helmut listened and grinned: "The Jewish blood will out."

Gisela had narrowly escaped a concentration camp. She is half Jewish.

I asked Helmut: "What do you mean when you say 'Jewish Blood'? Surely, it is no different from saying she is Italian, French, Greek or whatever."

"I am not sure." Helmut shrugged his shoulders.

"You know, sometimes I think it was people like us who killed the Jews. The way we used to talk: 'What a brilliant pianist, but then – of course – he is Jewish.' Or: 'He is the best surgeon I know. Naturally, one of the chosen race.' We were always setting them apart, we talked about them in a disparaging way."

"Oh, but they are different, you must agree." Helmut sounded unsure.

"That's exactly what Hitler said, exploiting the existing prejudice. It was easy then to rouse the masses. Not even he can have believed in his own propaganda that Jews were an inferior race. He feared them. They were, quite often, intellectually superior. Feared and distrusted them, because they carried their civilisation with them wherever they went. He could not conquer their country, only exterminate them individually."

"I understand what you are saying," Helmut smiled.

"Come, let's find Gisela and talk to her about your theories. She'll like that. You are a good friend."

9 p.m.

We get 90 Marks (the new German Deutsch Marks) for that suit, a fortune at this time in Germany.

Kiel *6 June 1949*

Today is our last day in Kiel. I watch Henning: tanned, but no longer as blond as he was in past years, his brown eyes alight with pleasure as Dick shows him a trick with cards, and I wonder: will he eventually be allowed to come to England? I can see years and years in front of me, travelling to Germany, pleading with my mother and Henning's father, seeing the disappointment in the boy's face. Years only of holidays with him, ending in countless sad goodbyes. He does not often talk about his step-mother. And I do not like to ask too many questions. "She's alright," he will say, "but she's very strict. Sometimes I have to wash up. And I mustn't be too loud. But really, she's very nice." That is not much to go by and I keep quiet. But it hurts, oh it hurts. I try to shake myself free of such thoughts. They will not go away, but I do not want the last day with him spoilt.

"Come on, let's go to the beach and catch some crabs for our supper."

I forced myself. Crab-catching had been a great pleasure for me during school holidays, staying with my aunt in Kiel.

"Right, where is the bucket?" Henning was already racing ahead of Dick and myself.

London *8 June 1949*

Suddenly it was all over. Goodbyes to Gisela and Helmut, our dearest friends, to my family with just a hint of sadness, but acceptance that understanding each other cannot go further, and then a long, dreary train journey with Henning, whom we had to hand over to his uncle in Solingen. From there he would be collected by his father. This uncle! How well I remember him, the vicar who conducted my marriage service and christened my son. When we reached the vicarage, I rang the bell and Henning suddenly pleaded: "You'd better go. He does not like you." Nor do I like him, but we stayed. The door opened, just a crack, and a familiar voice said, "Come in Henning, quickly," and shut again.

No time to give my boy a last hug, to remind him to write, to kiss him goodbye. I was shocked, and Dick's, "Well, I never . . ." was unmistakable.

"Come on, love. It doesn't really matter, does it? He'll always be your son." He put his arm round me, fumbled for a handkerchief to wipe away my tears and said in a firm voice: "Now for Cologne. Remember? You want to stop there to see the Rhine again, think of holidays with your father."

So, back to the station, on to an old, slow train taking us to Cologne. We had been travelling all through the night with Henning and felt very weary, we desperately needed some sleep.

In the Station Restaurant, over a coffee, I asked a waiter if he knew of any hotel nearby with a so-called dayroom.

"Before the war, one could have a room just for a few hours during the day. We've been on the train all night, we are extremely tired. Does this type of service still exist?"

Off he went, smiling broadly, and came back with a slip of paper.

"This should be alright," he said, and we set out to find the place, definitely not an easy task in Cologne. In comparison with Kiel and Hamburg which we had also visited, very briefly, and which had been reborn in a most spectacular way in a very short space of time, practically no reconstruction has taken place here. We still had to climb over heaps of rubble. There are incongruous piles of metal everywhere, boarded windows, hollow walls, and road signs for roads that are not really there. Part of the beautiful cathedral is destroyed, and a big bridge across the Rhine is even now half lying in water – a bewildering picture four years after the end of the war.

At last, we found the address the waiter had given us. We looked at each other: what on earth was that? It was not a hotel at all, just an ordinary, slightly derelict house. We rang the bell.

"Yes?" An elderly woman stood at the door.

"Have you got a dayroom?" Dick asked. His German is reasonably good by now.

"For how long?"

"Four to five hours, I think," he answered. "We are very tired."

"Come with me." She nodded. "That will be ten Marks in advance." We followed her along a dingy corridor to an equally dingy room. "You have to be out by three o'clock."

"Thank you." Dick paid and we sank into the beds, only to be awakened minutes later by arguments outside, followed by giggles and shrieks and repeated opening and shutting of doors.

"Good heavens," Dick groaned, "do you know in what sort of house we are?"

I had a shrewd idea. It did not matter. All I wanted was a good long sleep.

On the way home we were both very quiet, each with our own thoughts. It was inconceivable to me that the doomed cities of Germany would ever rise again. And yet, I saw with my own eyes what prodigious use the Germans made of the American aid offered. What faith there was in the enormous collective effort of my people.

Should I have stayed with them?

Poverty and pain are the real problems in the world, it seems to me. They have begun to conquer the first of them in such a short time, an astonishing achievement. And the pain? The pain is of uncertainty. I am pessimistic: the chronic instability, the absence of a centre of national gravity that gives to any nation self-assurance and prevents its people from embarking on frantic, passionate ventures has hardly lessened. Hitler had given the Germans a goal, although it had been the wrong one. It had to be replaced.

It is probably far too early to foresee what can happen. For the time being there are only four occupied zones, no German nation. The Russians are in the land East of the river Elbe, and in the West the Americans get the scenery, the French the wine and the British the ruins. That is a bitter joke, but it is true. The British Zone covers the most densely populated and incredibly ravaged areas of Germany, including the industrial Ruhr and the most important port, Hamburg. I feel that probably for many years to come Britains will live there as conquerors, in a country many of them know very little about. Thinking back to the time after the war when I worked for the Control Commission, and reliving the last two weeks, when I had been watching and talking to British people, I have come to the conclusion that there are now even more ex-colonial staff in Kiel and Hamburg than in 1946/7, almost as if, to solve the immediate problems of the country, they had turned to their experience of colonial administration. Are they considered to have a suitable background? Perhaps they had brought the attitude with them that they are the colonial power and the Germans the natives? Although the clock has started again for the Germans in 1948, when a currency reform launched a return to normality and to the beginnings of economic revival, the relationship between critical British and German people is still somewhat strained and mistrustful.

I felt this very much when, one day during our visit, we were invited into the flat of a Kiel journalist, a friend of Gisela's and Helmut's. He was young and passionately nationalistic. He could not understand my leaving the country.

"We need people like you. You could have helped the British to understand us."

"But I have," I looked at Dick, "and I still do although on the other side, as you may say. I think I am doing a good job in England, for all of you."

"What? Don't make me laugh!"

"Look, English interests and yours agree in many ways."

"But surely, the people over there dislike us intensely?"

I looked at the young German and shook my head, a little sad.

"No, I am sure you are wrong. There is little illwill amongst them towards Germans generally. I should know. I have hardly met any."

"I am sorry, I can't believe you."

"You ought to hear the British talk about the French!"

I was carried away on a tide of emotion: "The killing is over. Love will always prove stronger than hatred."

Nobody said anything for a moment, then he replied: "Perhaps you are right. I should not see you as an outsider. We have much to learn. And the worsening in relations between the Russians and the West ought to bring us together. There have to be new alignments. After all, what does it mean, 'winning a war'? I have heard about austerity in England." There certainly is.

Halfway across the Channel, approaching Dover, I took a deep breath. Enough now. Roy was expecting us at his grandmother's, our home was waiting for us and I was returning to interesting work.

All good positive thoughts, a rich useful life I had chosen, and a husband to support me. Reason enough to feel happy. We smiled at each other. He understands the agony of separation from Henning, the sadness I feel about my family, hopes I have for Germany.

"Remember? I am here, and we are going home now. Roy and I need you badly. You do belong here."

I love him, but I cried.

11 September 1949

Gisela has given us the address of a Jewish great aunt of

hers who had been fortunate enough to emigrate to London before the outbreak of war and had settled in Hendon. I have written to her and now have received an invitation to visit her.

A very elegant old lady she is! Afternoon tea, and she is presiding as if she is holding court. It is like stepping into Germany way in the past. There are several ex-Germans there and the talk is all about Germany: "That hat, and the handbag, do they come from Germany? Do you speak German at home? Have you been to Covent Garden to see this year's Wagner operas?"

This is the last thing I want to do! I am very fond of the 'Mastersingers' and 'The Flying Dutchman', but any of the 'Ring' operas makes me think of Hitler's adoration of Teutonic ideas, and signature tunes on the radio during the war, snatched from Wagner themes. I stopped that line of thinking: it would not be the same to these people. They remember glamorous Wagner events when they were respected citizens of 'their' country, sitting in expensive seats, not only enjoying the theatrical spectacle but the social gathering as well. They could not be affected by Wagner's music like myself. They had left the country before his music was misused. I did not answer their question.

"You have lived in Berlin, you say. What is it like now?" I do not know. I have not been there since 1943, and now it is cut off from the world by Russian intervention. Only the air lift of supplies into

Germany's old capital in 1948 has saved the town from starvation and possible surrender to the Russians. I looked at the old lady: "Berlin, I don't know, we were only allowed to visit Kiel and Hamburg, but I can tell you, there is so much going on and the Germans are working very hard to make good. Old trustworthy politicians are trying to restructure the country, trying to make the Allies see that they want to be part of the Western Alliance, that they can be relied upon."

She sighed: "Just the same, I never want to go back again, not now."

Several of the guests nodded in agreement; I was silent. What could I say? I have returned to England with visions of at least half a nation emerging from a daze, with impressions of vigour and courage, and I have come back with a love for my old country which can quite happily exist by the side of my new love: England. But I too, like those sad, disillusioned German Jews, have no desire to live in Germany again.

Saturday *8 October 1949*

This morning I handed Dick the *News Chronicle* and pointed out to him a little notice about Cologne.

"This is really funny, look," I laughed. "Do you remember the bridge half in the Rhine? The rubble and ruins? Not many people involved in cleaning the roads?"

"Do I remember Cologne?" He winked at me and read about Adenauer's problems. Konrad Adenauer, the past Lord Mayor of Cologne and now the first Kanzler (Prime Minister) of the Federal Republic of Germany, one of the leading fighters against National Socialism had thought it much more important to restore the morale of his citizens by spending vast sums of money, paid by the American Marshall Aid, on the legendary Cologne Carnival rather than do what other cities had done: rebuild as quickly as possible. This I understand, being half Rhenish. The people along the Rhine had lived through especially terrible years. So let them enjoy being alive. Adenauer is Rhenish as well. His problem? The Allies do not approve that mentality and are very ignorant about the Cologne Carnival, causing political problems for the great old man.

15 October 1949

The morning mail brought a letter from Joyce's mother. I was surprised and touched. It is nearly two years ago that I stood on her doorstep and was, not very politely, turned away. She asks me to visit her.

> "You have been such a good friend of my daughter's, and I have never forgotten meeting you. I am still ashamed about my outburst then, and today I can no longer understand what made me be so unkind towards somebody who

had no share in what happened to my family. Please forgive me."

We talked on the telephone. A little later I went to see her. I understand. I like her. Perhaps she will become a maternal friend? Time is a great healer.

I know that Joyce's mother is a simple woman from London's Eastend. I should have thought of that when she refused to welcome me into her house. She lacks the frequently artificial subtlety of so-called good manners. She had simply spoken her mind on that occasion. I, on the other hand, being at that time constantly on guard against possible hostile reception, had overreacted and caused myself unnecessary pain. Now I can look at that incident in a much calmer, impartial way.

At the same time, a question flashing through my mind hits me violently and renews my doubts: *she* did not know how to disguise her feelings. How many people have I met in the meantime who knew very well how to do just that? How many of our so-called friends were honestly accepting me for what I am, how many were mainly curious and were, behind my back, shrugging their shoulders, saying: "Well, you know how it is. She is quite interesting, but she *is* German. So, what do you expect. Of course, Dick is a nice fellow . . ."

I do not want to probe any more. I fight that idea. I do so want to feel at home with everyone of them, to know they truly like me as a person, never mind where I came from.

17 October 1949

All those boring old chemical processes have been translated. Thank goodness! I am qualified to do the type of work, but what a tedious job it was. The research chemist, who is in charge of the project, told me one morning that the work is finished.

"Good," I said with heartfelt gratitude.

"No more of this now," he continued, "but if you like to stay with us – secretarial work, you know; you must have learned a lot about chemistry during the last months." He looked slightly embarrassed. – "You see, the fact of the matter is – now you'll think this is a joke – we already know all the papers are outdated. It is funny, isn't it?"

It certainly is. Nearly a year's work, a year's money, and now such a result! We both laughed and laughed.

"Come on," he said, "I'll buy you a drink and lunch."

And we went to a cosy little pub off the Stratford Market, where I told him that I wanted to move on to do something else or, perhaps, even stay at home for a while. I do not know yet, only that it has to be something new, something different again. Always restless, always searching.

"We will keep in touch, won't we?" he smiled at me.

"Of course we will. I hate losing friends like you."

29 October 1949

We were sitting in Lyon's Cornerhouse in Leicester Square, enjoying a meal after half a day's shopping in the West End. It was impossible not to overhear the gentlemen sitting at the next table. Officials of some kind. They were talking of German Civil Servants who were to be invited to study local government on the spot.

"They have to be put in private houses," one of them said. "It's too expensive otherwise. There have been very few offers so far."

We listened, and I whispered to Dick: "That sounds interesting. Shall we join in?"

And we did. The officials were very pleased when we offered to take someone in for a fortnight. They then explained who these people are, exactly, and what they will be doing here. They are a new generation of German town officials, politically cleared, who will be shown round English Town Halls to see how the various departments work. They will attend lectures – if necessary in German – and will receive information on the intricacies of British Trade Unions. They are not all young people; some of them have been involved in local government before the war. I feel very enthusiastic. It would be nice to have a German lady in the house. It could be another chance for building bridges. The officials will send us details.

15 November 1949

The days are cold and dark once again. It is nice to sit by the fire at home. Sometimes I enjoy not having to go out to work. There are nice ways of spending cold days at home.

I brought back old photos of friends and family from our visit to Germany. A precious present my mother gave me. Marianne and I had been forced to leave all our belongings behind when we fled from Austria. I had no pictures of Henning as a small child, no photos of friends nor my parents. Amongst the snapshots were a few of a group of my old schoolfriends. What has become of them? Some contacts I had been able to make soon after the war, other friends stayed in the Russian Zone and were – for the time being, anyway – lost to me.

In Germany, our class reunions had been more than a sentimental journey into the past. During the school years it had been very important to everyone in the same form seemingly to be in control of life and to be amenable. There had hardly ever been a serious conversation, nobody admitted they thought about anything other than their school work and their social life. So often we had been pretending in our relationships. Small talk had kept us safe. Some of our lives were laid out in advance by the rules of our time, but later the rules and the social customs that shaped our lives had changed.

There was Marlies, who had become a pharmacist, married, and lost her husband within the first three months of married life; Ursula with two children, her husband fell in Russia. There was Ruth who studied law, she fell in love with an impoverished German count and married him. His title, I think, played a big part in this decision. He was a playboy, always in debt and, when she could not support him any longer, he left her. At the end of the war she found her mother in the East. Her two brothers and her father, all doctors in the Army, had died near Stalingrad. Later I heard that she settled in Leipzig, came to terms with the political system in the German Democratic Republic and made a name for herself as a solicitor. Hanna became a nurse and married a doctor who was killed after the war when he tried to escape from a Russian POW camp. Marie-Louise came from a large, poor family. Her father's advice had always been: "Never be without money. It is the most important thing in the world." She was a beautiful girl, so it was not too difficult to find a rich, though much older man as a husband. He died a few years later. She had all the wealth anyone could wish for, but she was very lonely. They were *all* lonely, with little to look forward to. Some rebuilt their careers to fill that void and to support their children, others eventually found a niche for themselves and spent their pensions for war-widows and refugees on travelling and visiting, forever in search of constancy.

None of them married again. So very few young men had returned from the war.

Sunday *27 November 1949*

Frau Wolf has arrived. I have prepared our guest room, put flowers and a box of chocolates by her bedside (as I feel sure, one would still do in Germany), and have, on this cold and wet November evening, a big casserole cooking in the oven.

She is about forty years old, friendly, but a little shy, mainly because her English is restricted. However, when she found out that I am German and that Dick speaks the language, the stream of questions became endless. I wanted her to feel at home, so I asked, as I have been asked many times in England: "What is your Christian name? Mine is Pat."

"Oh no, please," she appeared puzzled and embarrassed, "Frau Wolf."

That is obviously too much for her. She finds it impossible to jump this particular hurdle. The Germans' love of formality is too strong. The 'Anglo-Saxon ease' our friend Gisela often teases us about in slightly envious tones, evades her. So, 'Frau Wolf' and 'Frau Skinner' it is and remains.

Her husband had been considered politically unreliable and, although not Jewish, died in prison. She feels, with a very strong sense of duty, that she owes it to him to assist in the rebirth of her country. And she works very hard while she stays with us. In the evenings I help her with her English homework, and I hope that in a small way I can bring about closer relations between our two countries.

25 February 1950

The other morning, a blonde, very friendly looking woman stood in front of me at the butcher's.

"One and a half pounds of beef," she said.

I detected a strong guttural German accent.

"What sort of beef, Madam?"

"For cooking, of course."

"Yes, but what do you want: for braising, roasting?"

"No, cooking. You know, slow cooking, on the stove."

"I'm sorry, there is no stewing beef today."

"What? With so many cows here?" She pointed, in a vague way, to the meat hanging up in the shop. The other customers were not pleased. I could read their thoughts showing in the way they smiled. "Ignorant foreigners . . ."

I caught up with her, a little later, as she was walking home, in the direction I was going.

"I heard you in the shop. You are German, aren't you?"

She stopped dead: "Yes, oh yes, you too? I am Maria, and you?"

"My name is Pat."

"Hello, Pat. It is nice of you to stop me."

We walked together part of our way home, and she started talking about herself. She was widowed in the war and, after marrying a British soldier, came to England with her small daughter. She speaks little English, she is a simple girl from the Ruhr area of Germany, but makes a valiant effort to create a new family in a new country. She is determined to accept and understand England: she also encourages her daughter to learn and establish herself in her new surroundings, which she does very successfully.

She most certainly does not belong to the German Brides Club of Romford.

Maria became my first German friend in England. It is very important to me. She is warmhearted, with a sunny disposition. We compare notes. She accepts everything new or different more readily than I do. I probe and want to know why. She'll laugh and say: "Come on, when in Rome . . . Why do you sometimes make it so hard for yourself?" Yes, why? And at once the pain, most times well controlled, rushes to the surface: She has her child by her side, I left mine behind.

I help Maria in improving her English, and she meets our friends which, in some cases, means a new bond and yet another step towards finding a new identity and forming ties with English and German people alike, both friends for life.

I smile to myself, remembering an English anecdote somebody told me a long time ago:

> An Englishman was asked: "Whom do you like best? The French, Germans, Italians, Americans?" Each time he shook his head and

said 'no'. "I don't understand, answered the inquisitor, you must like somebody. Do you only like English people?"
"Not at all," the Englishman replied. "I like my friends."

If I think back to the darkest and brightest hours of my days, it was the strong thread of friendship weaving through my life that helped me over difficult times and enhanced the good ones. There was Marianne, my sister, during the war years, but that thought hurts. I have lost her. There were two or three friends I could talk to about my dilemma when I had decided to leave Germany; I could feel their warmth and understanding, they never changed towards me. And, in my life in England now, there are new close friends. In good times friendship means giving and receiving; in times of need it becomes an anchor. I have never found it to be a flame, rather a steady, reliable pilot light.

7 March 1950

I was awakened by a slanting ray of sun flooding my bed and putting an end to confused, frightening dreams. Suddenly, I was wide awake, startled. My mother. I dreamt about her. She sat by the open window, as I have so often seen her, her face serious and pale, very pale.

"Have you done the right thing?" she asked. "Can you honestly say to me you are happy? Have you no regrets?"

She had asked similar questions in her letters. Why do I feel so disturbed? And all of a sudden, with a jolt, I realise why: she spoke to me in English, she, who did not know any English at all.

"What's the matter," Dick asked over breakfast. "You look terrible. Something wrong?"

"I am alright, I just didn't sleep very well." I did not look at him. He is very perceptive to my moods. I couldn't tell him anything at that moment. I waited until he went to work and Roy was on his way to school. Then I rang my sister. It took such a long time to get a connection to Kiel, I felt very tense.

"Marianne? How are you all? I don't know why, but I am worried."

"Why should you be?" she retorted. Normally you don't care much what happens here." Her voice was very cold.

"But I do, and you know it. I keep on writing and sending things. Why do you cut me off? How is mother?"

"Not very well," her voice softened. "There have been tests during the last two weeks. We don't know yet."

"What is it? I'm coming home."

"Don't be silly," she argued, "You belong there now. She is in good hands. I am a nurse, after all, or have you forgotten?"

I cringed. Of course I know my mother will be looked after very well by my sister, whatever her illness is, but I urgently want to see for myself.

"I'm coming as soon as I can organise it." I nearly shouted into the telephone. And then I couldn't wait until Dick came home. I rang him in his office.

"Do you think I can go to Kiel?" I asked.

"Yes, darling, we can all go in the summer. We planned to, remember?"

"No, I don't mean that. I mean now, sorry, I don't know, mother is ill."

"Alright, calm down. I'm coming home straightaway and we will talk if it is that urgent."

That is Dick, a rock. I did not tell him about the dream. I was, maybe, frightened that he would make light of that. I simply said I felt the need to ring Marianne. And from then on he took over. He is so supportive. I may appear to be in control, but I really am not. In his retiring way he is for ever watchful, concerned. I love him for this.

Kiel — *11 March 1950*

I arrived in Kiel to see my mother in bed, very fragile and ash-grey, her dark eyes intense as I walked into her room.

"I am glad you have come. Will you stay?"

What did she mean? For good? I did not give her an

answer, but asked how she was. She waived that and said: "Let's talk about more important things, let's talk about you."

I nodded.

"Can you honestly tell me you are happy? No regrets?"

I was stunned. Those had been her very words in my dream and suddenly we were very close, all bitterness gone. Perhaps I had been wrong: family bonds *are* always there though circumstances change. Here is a kind of telepathic contact that makes me very happy.

"Yes, mother, yes. And I am sorry I caused you so much heartache."

She smiled, a sad smile.

"Perhaps I did not always understand you. I wanted the best for you, but my ways were not yours. I think I was wrong about Dick, too."

She lay back. "You wrote about building bridges. I am too old. I just want peace. I want to live – if I am going to live – with old memories of you and Marianne, of some good years between the wars. I know there were many things we did not know anything about, during the Hitler years I mean, but I am too old now to analyse them and to try solving some of the questions. Your father is different; I am very, very tired."

Father came into the room.

"He knows," she said. "He is very sure about you and trusts your judgement."

I turned to him and he led me away.

"I believe you made her very happy by coming to see her." He stroked my hair. "But she must rest now. We'll go in again later."

Marianne remained distant.

"Come and see us," I pleaded with her. "You'll change your mind about England, perhaps even about Dick and me. Don't the war years we spent together mean anything to you? We used to be such a good team."

"Maybe," she replied, "but you have moved too far away."

I am only staying in Kiel for a few days. There is nothing I can do, Marianne is in charge. I have a strong, sad feeling that perhaps I shall never see my mother again. How strange it is, there has never been, in my memory, the warmth of a good relationship between my parents, and yet now my father seems to lean heavily on my mother's greater mental strength, appears lost and utterly helpless, simply waiting for her to recover, hoping she will take over again.

London *18 March 1950*

In my sleep I dream. This has always been so. From a shadowy background scenes of startling clarity emerge, in brilliant colours. As a young girl I had sometimes talked about my dreams in the morning, over breakfast, but I was always slightly resentful when father and mother smiled with mild indulgence.

Now I cannot say anything. The dreams have become sad ones, they might hurt Dick, they might make him question my happiness. Many of them fade, but the pictures of childhood remain: a warm summer evening on the balcony, with father smoking a pipe, radio music in the background; a dark night when, waking with great fear that there was some sinister being in the room, I ran from my own bed to another, close to father or mother, and was comforted; remembrance of sorrow, but I do not know why I am sad, of an immense longing, but I do not know for what. Time and again I wake up crying, but do not understand the reason.

My life is reflected by the life of dreams. Weird, misty sometimes, frighteningly sharp at others. Reflections of reality. Often I try to will myself not to dream of Henning, the son I left behind.

That dream about my mother has become a turning-point. Have I been taken over? Now, quite frequently, in my dreams old German friends, father or Marianne talk in English to me. To think in English has become normal, but to dream in a foreign language? Is this the final stage? We hardly ever speak German at home and, if so, sometimes for fun mixed with English. Amazing really that, from the start of our visits to Kiel, German phrases came easily. I was suspicious and listened to myself: no accent? No English word order in German sentences? I am relieved. I do not want to add to my misdeeds in the eyes of my family.

3 April 1950

There have been so many changes, so many ups and downs over the last three years in my relationships with Roy but, gradually, I feel confident in understanding him. I love this vivacious, dark-eyed boy who will now come home from school, hug me, fall over himself to grab milk and biscuits and then disappear in the park to join his friends. "No homework today, Mummy," he will shout, although I do not always believe him. He will not be a great academic, but is full of love for sport, nature and animals.

The other day he came home from school, with a kitten in his arms. "I found him by the side of the road, in a shrub. He was terrified and miaowed. Can I keep him?"

This is in addition to a hamster in the shed and the grave of a crow. The crow – that is a different story. He had shot it, on his uncle Ken's farm in Essex, and had brought it home in a cardboard box to show us, then to bury it in the garden, only to be dug up half a dozen times to prove to his friends what he had done. And now it was a kitten, jet black, hungry looking, with green eyes.

"We'll try," I said, "he may run away."

"I'll call him Caesar!" Roy was jubilant. "I like that name." Of course he does. He likes reading and, at present, there is nothing more exciting than the lives of Roman heroes.

"Let's take him to the vet," I suggested today, "he'll have to be inoculated."

Roy put him into a big carton and off we went to the vet we have discovered in the neighbourhood. We both entered the surgery, and a very embarrassed Roy had to adjust himself when the vet said: "This is no Caesar, son, this is a Cleopatra." However for him she remains Caesar.

Roy's trust in me has grown during the last three years. I am always apprehensive when he returns from staying with his mother. He is very quiet then, moody in games and home-work, staying in his room, wanting to be alone. I understand and feel certain that Henning, after spending some time with me, would react similarly. They have lived consciously through the last hard years of the war and remembered. Soon after that the family ties were severed. They need much time to cope with the big changes in their young lives.

Children born after the war are much more outgoing, reliant and confident. To them, the war is in the past and they can feel free of fear and hopeful. These children seem to know they are safe. The horror their parents suffered does no longer exist and does not transfer itself to the children.

Roy has developed into a self-assured boy, fond of games but not too enthusiastic about school work.

"Eventually he'll have to sit for the 'Eleven plus'." Dick was thinking aloud. "We could afford to send him to a Prep School. He would get more attention, work in small groups."

"To be away for weeks on end?" I was stunned, I had never known a boarding school in Germany, and the thought of sending a small boy away from home to be looked after by unknown people appalled me for a moment. It does not make sense to me to pay a lot of money, perhaps more than we can afford, to be relieved of a child we love. And that for the best part of the year.

"I don't want to push him out, but he will learn so much more about himself. Remember, he is an only child. There he will live with other boys, he will be in a team all the time. That is important."

Yes, I know. And the feeling of recurring anguish is back: we still have no child of our own.

"I think a good answer would be if he were a weekly boarder. Then he would be home every weekend. Do you like that better?"

Dick did not give up easily, and I do not want any change. Life with Roy is good.

"Perhaps St John's near Chelmsford. A colleague of mine has his son there. I think they take boys in summer as well. I'll find out."

Slowly I resigned myself to the idea. No more waiting for him outside the school, looking at his shiny, flushed face when he had been playing games and had won a race, no more 'can Martin come home with us? His mum will be late'. After the slow, upward battle to win his confidence and trust I am a little frightened of how much I shall miss him. He, however, is excited. "You will look after Caesar for me, won't you?"

April 1950

And so Roy has entered St John's Preparatory School. After a short chat with the headmaster we handed him over to his housemaster who took him away to join the other new ones in the gym, all of them in short black trousers, red blazers and caps. I have got used to school uniforms now, unknown in Germany. We followed but are politely asked to leave and have a word with the matron whom we – no doubt, he says – would want to meet. Yes, I did want to speak to her, tell her about myself, the stepmother, his fear of being left alone, his dislike of certain foods. When we found her, she just smiled, a gentle understanding smile: "All parents are the same. Don't worry too much. We'll take good care of him."

We returned to the gym, wanting to say goodbye to our boy, who suddenly seemed so small and vulnerable. We called out to him. He did not come running towards us, but stayed with the other boys, gave us a big grin and shouted: "Bye, bye, see you at the weekend," turning his attention once more to his newly found friends. I could not believe it. I know I'll miss him terribly. But I'll need to learn to cope again.

5 May 1950

Two and a half years ago I knew practically nothing about gardening and now know very little more, although our garden has become very important to me. I have time this spring and always long to fill the gap Roy's absence creates. What better way to do that than spending warm, sunny spring days amongst our new roses. We replaced the stolen ones very soon after we moved in. I never thought I would be able to plant roses successfully and feel very proud and vastly encouraged. I watch and count the buds, daily, willing them to burst into flower, very soon now.

This year there is a little rockery in one corner of the garden. Dick built the foundations – his only contribution to gardening apart from mowing the lawn – and I coax Primroses, Violas, Alyssum and Aubrietia, also some Dwarf Phlox, along lovingly. For the moment it looks a little like a giant's grave. Something is wrong. Never mind, the Hollyhocks against the neighbour's garden are beginning to grow and the shrubs look healthy. I do not even know their names yet, apart from two big purple and white lilac bushes, flowering each year at the time of my birthday. Wherever there was a little space, I planted Pansies, in brilliant colours, together with Marigolds and Pinks. An expert might frown and think how much more could be done and how much better the garden could look. But, for a would-be gardener like me, who never before sat in her own garden, it is sheer paradise. Every morning going out, anxiously looking if my tiny plants have grown a little, fighting weeds which, to my mind, are often as pretty as the real flowers and then, later on a sunny day, taking a book and a deckchair, a sandwich and fruit for lunch to my lavender corner, wondering if it will be as blue and lovely as last summer.

I am very happy. Today is Tuesday, only three more days and Roy will be home for the weekend, probably ravaging the odd flower bed with his football.

6 June 1950

Taking Roy to school after the half-term break he said: "Today is blub day, blub Sunday."

"What? Why?"

"It's the new ones. They cry because it is the first week-end they are away from home. They hide. We find them and give them a bit of a bashing."

"But that is terrible!"

"It isn't, not really. The same thing happened to me when I came here. Over there, under the bushes. I hid there, and they found me."

"And today you are going to look for somebody like that?"

"Sure. I know there are one or two hiding. And I know where. Like myself last term. Only, I cried hardly at all."

The idea of democratic education for British children? First I get a hiding, then I'll give you one. Is this the same little boy who used to be terrified of thunderstorms? When, one night, a violent storm woke him and he came running into our bedroom, I made him stand at the French windows with me and tried to tell him how beautiful such a sight was and, in a simple way, why there were thunderstorms.

"I'll give you sixpence if you stay here with me and just watch." He did, but cried out once or twice.

"There," I hugged him, "it is nearly over. You needn't be afraid."

"I am still, a little," he swallowed. "Do you think it was worth twopence?"

I become used to the rhythm of our week now, both of us look forward to Friday night. Roy does as well, and every weekend feels like a little bit of Christmas.

We make sure we are free to spend all Saturday and Sunday with him, go swimming, occasionally watch the local Cricket team or, if the weather is bad, go to a cinema. Sometimes one or two of his 'old' school friends come for tea. That can be critical, though: He wants them to come, but is inclined to boast a little about his new school. We have to tread gently here and steer the boys away from the subject, not to hurt Martin or Julian.

The weekend passes very quickly, but every time he leaves for the week it becomes a little easier for me. For Dick as well? He never talks about it.

4 July 1950

Yesterday, Peggy, Roy's mother, telephoned and asked to see us. She and her husband would like to talk to us, but without Roy being present. It sounded very important. Of course we agreed and arranged to meet tonight. I was very curious and slightly nervous while we waited for them. I like them both, but I sensed that there was something unusual in that call.

When they arrived the atmosphere was rather cold. We all tried to smile, but it felt wrong. I tried to help them, and they went straight to the point. There is a very good position waiting for them in Australia and they wonder what our reaction would be if they were to take Roy with them.

"But you did not want him!" Dick was quite sharp; I had never heard him like that before.

She looked at both of us and went on to explain that she has felt guilty about it ever since she left Roy. And, most important: "It would be a brand new life for all of us." They have a little daughter too. That hurt even more. We still have not been able to start a family of our own.

All the time I was thinking how I would miss Roy. But I did not know how to answer.

Dick was very serious: "I never understood why you left him. Can you tell us now?"

And she did. She said that Roy was too much like his father, and that she could not bear to see him when they separated. She wanted to be free, and Dick gave her that freedom. There was silence for a moment.

Then I broke in: "What about Roy? Shouldn't we ask him?" I wanted to say how much he meant to Dick – and to me – but very little came out. I felt utterly miserable.

"This is why we wanted to see you without Roy." Peggy's husband said.

Still nobody said much. But we agreed to their coming back this Saturday, when Roy is here. By then we will have thought about it too. Dick did not say anything after Peggy left. I know he needs time. I long to say, "Please don't let him go," but I know I must not influence Dick on decisions of this kind. I also know that Dick is so uncompromisingly fair that he will let Roy make the decision. I think I know what it will be.

And I dread it.

8 July 1950

I shall never forget the radiant pleasure in Roy's face when he burst into the lounge with a jubilant, "You are all here! Hello, Mummy." He hugged Peggy, his dark eyes alight. Yes, that is his Mummy. I am his Mum. I swallowed hard. My eyes were burning.

Dick told Roy why we were all together, and what Peggy's plans were. There was a moment of silence, a sigh and then Roy simply said: "I'd like that. Will you really take me?" And, turning to Dick, "Can I?"

What could Dick say? The big trip, the idea of wallabies and kangaroos, sheep and cattle stations right out of comic books play an important part in Roy's decision. But the most important reason, no doubt, is that his mother wants him back. And there is the baby sister as well. I did not matter at that moment. I have only been the caretaker. As if the boy sensed my distress, he turned to me and said, very seriously: "You don't mind, do you? Perhaps Henning will come. I'll write to you."

That is what Henning had said. But what are letters against the crying need to have a child in the house, to play with, to hold and comfort when he is unhappy? Dick's child or mine, it is not important. I felt drained. What would I do? I left the room and busied myself in the kitchen, making tea. What else?

20 August 1950

Dick settled all matters concerning Roy's school (so much for the Eleven-plus!), I prepared his trunk, and off he went. The day he left, perhaps for good, in his short black trousers, red blazer and cap has been the saddest in my English life, so far.

The saddest wedding anniversary as well. Roy left on the 8th, and it has taken us some time to recover. Dick and I have not talked much about it. We have to adapt now to our new role of being childless. We are generally very compatible and work as a good team – a duo? But there are great areas of differences, though I believe that a caring relationship solves this problem with a lot of understanding.

We have tried to go out more often. But there are big

differences between his taste and choice and mine. No opera for Dick, hardly any musicals, both of which I love. Instead, always a historic drama, a thriller or a comedy for him.

I was fascinated by the reviews of a new play, described as 'hilariously funny', praising Richard Attenborough's performance. I know him, I have seen him in war films. Both of us needed a happy, carefree evening after the distress of Roy's departure. This did look like a nice surprise for my husband. Saturday night at the Savoy Theatre. I booked two tickets and told him.

"Oh, nice. What is it called?"

"To Dorothy, a son," I said. He looked startled.

"What?" I repeated. "Pat, what do you mean to tell me?"

"No, no!" I hastened to destroy any illusions he might have. Did he think I chose the title of this play to tell him I am pregnant? We do not talk about children of our own any longer. It hurts too much. Occasionally I still consider myself a guest in somebody's home and fear such a feeling will stay with me unless I have a child in this country. I can claim entitlement to roots then, if that time ever comes. Although we are, I fear, resigned to the fact that we cannot have this wish fulfilled.

A slight pause, and then: "Would you really like a son again? I mean if . . . It would be wonderful to have a daughter, don't you agree? Another little woman about the house?"

"I don't know. I have a strong feeling that I would be better as a boy's mother but, of course, it would not matter. Dick, I . . ." and in sudden despair I burst out: "This is only a play, it is supposed to be very good, please don't say any more."

"It's alright." He sat on the rest of my armchair and bent over me. "I am sorry. Let's forget it."

21 August 1950

We went out and had a beautiful evening together. Standing in the bar, drink in hand like nearly everybody else, I was as always surprised at English theatre-goers. They appear in every variety of sloppiness: women barelegged or in trousers, with scarlet toenails showing through open sandals, men in pullovers, lots of people smoking – which I have seen before in the auditorium as well – enjoying being part of a crowd. In Germany, theatre had meant dark suits for the men, elegant dresses and even gloves sometimes for the women, and above all, subdued orderly walking in the foyer during intervals, watching out for people one knew. That was important. Everybody wanted to be seen.

Red toenails. I like that. I must try one day.

Coming out of the theatre, we were still laughing. It really was a very good comedy, but there is one thing I cannot understand. Why don't people applaud more? The actors played superbly, there was so much laughter around us and, in the end, the cast received two or three curtain calls. Three! In Germany they would have had seven or eight. And flowers. It is not fair. Actors thrive on recognition. Here, everybody seems anxious to get away quickly. Why?

At first, he had no explanation for this.

"Perhaps it is all part of English reticence in showing their feelings," he reflected in the end. "Maybe they are in a hurry to catch a bus or a tube."

Sometimes he can be infuriating.

10 October 1950

A first letter from Roy! He is living in Adelaide now. Both of us have been waiting for mail from him, but carefully avoided mentioning it. Dick tore the letter open, then stopped and smiled:

"Come, we'll read it together."

There was not much in it. What does a ten year old say? He was fine, school was not important, but swimming and sailing were. Francis, the baby sister, was naughty and funny, and: 'how is Caesar?'

'I love you both.' he wrote. 'I'll write again soon.'

There was also a brief note from Peggy to say that he had settled easily and enjoyed outdoor life.

'Hello Pat and Dick,' she wrote, 'Roy is happy and well

and adores little Francis. We are very grateful. I can imagine how hard it was for you to let him go. We'll send some photos for Christmas.'

Photos. They do not fill the gap. For a while, neither of us said anything, until Dick broke the silence:

"This won't do. Roy decided, we accepted it. We ought to be very pleased that he is happy. After all, aren't we?"

He tried. He did not quite convince me at that moment.

22 January 1951

We still have not been able to fill the house with children, but on the other hand we have developed a taste for playing hosts to a number of young Germans. They are much more approachable and open-minded, and far more ready to accept differences between the two nations, but also see the chances for mutual understanding, than the older generation of Germans had been after the war.

Michael, a young law student on an English course is staying with us. He caused hilarious laughter one evening in our garden when he demonstrated how he was trained – still at school – to be a child soldier, exercising a spade with great skill. Luckily for him, hostilities came to an end before he had to put his training into practice. I did not want to stop him, but I did feel very nervous. What if neighbours were watching us? Something sinister going on in the 'German' house? A show like this could be very confusing to them. Besides, Michael is very tall, blonde and Germanic looking.

Before him we had Hix, who is training as a nurse. She works in a psychiatric hospital. And we also had Ursula, my German god-daughter. Having finished her studies in Germany, she came to stay with us to study English and to try to become proficient in the English language.

These frequent visits are good for Dick and me. Dick not only learn more German, but also a lot about German ways which he could not possibly have understood in the turbulent post-war period when he lived in Kiel.

I feel I have lost some of my 'steel-corset' when conversation switches to Hitler's time. Now I find myself speaking up without feeling as if I was being accused personally. I begin to see the curiosity in people's questions rather than to sense imputations of guilt. I see that now, from this safe position, I am able to help visiting Germans understand the English way of life.

Does it really matter that no German would cut potatoes with a knife? And that an English person would never use such an instrument to break a roll? Are English people more egocentric than Germans because they spell 'I' with a capital letter, whereas the German language gives the 'you' that distinction? And a very academic question which causes arguments without any of us being able to answer it: is the German theory of pronouncing Latin the only valid one? At least that is something we all laugh about.

All of our German friends like the ease with which people talk in a bar, often at a bus stop or in a shop, and the occasionally very superficial chat after formal introduction, not immediately enquiring 'what are you doing?' As had happened to Dick in Germany.

"Which Technical University have you been to?" he was asked.

"None," he answered. "I went through an apprenticeship and worked my way up."

After a very short time the German left him standing on his own.

We have had British visitors as well. Major Ferguson came to stay with us for a few days, just after Christmas. That crude, often drunk Scot who for a time, while I was working as an interpreter for the British Control

Commission in Kiel in 1945/6, was the Commanding Officer of the town. At that time I feared him, loathed him for his blunt, discourteous ways of dealing with British and German personnel alike. He was utterly unpredictable. At the same time, I had a sneaking admiration for a gallant officer who fought very bravely during the African campaign and was highly decorated. Occasionally I wondered if his brusque manners were merely his way of shielding himself against close contact with anybody. He must have seen hell during the war.

Dick understands and likes him. I do not. So, when he rang and told us he was in London, Dick invited him to come to us. I could not argue, not really, and when he arrived I took a deep breath.

"Hello, Pat!" A wide grin split his big, ruddy face, topped with curly red hair. "Nice to see you, as pretty as ever."

"Hello, Donald," I said, and thought: 'Please, don't kiss me.' Good, he did not.

He is a civilian now and, thank goodness, more moderate and never drunk. As far as I am concerned, he is pleasant but, apparently, considers me to be 'only' a German, looks forward to a big breakfast all ready and waiting for him when he comes down in the morning, and puts his shoes outside his bedroom door, obviously expecting them to be cleaned, hardly by Dick. I simply ignore that. I am now the wife of an Englishman, he is no longer a C.O. So what? I am a British subject as well.

It is a silent battle. In the end I won. The shoes were no longer there. Instead, he asked one morning where I keep cleaning materials for them.

He is an interesting man, though, and can tell gripping stories and funny episodes of the last war and previous encounters abroad before that. He had served in India for a long time.

And he is grateful to us. Perhaps he is very lonely. We do not know much about him, other than that he has a wife somewhere in Scotland. He never talks about his private life.

One evening he said: "I've booked a table at the 'Veraswami' for tomorrow night. Do you know it? I'd like to take you out for dinner."

We did not, and he explained that it is a well-known Indian restaurant in Regent Street. We were delighted. I had never eaten Indian food before. When we arrived, we were immediately transferred into a different world. The whole of the interior decor was elaborately eastern. All the personnel were dressed in colourful trousers, turbans, the Sikhs among them with their hair knotted on the top of their heads, the women in saris.

Donald scoffed at the sight, when I remarked how beautiful I found it.

"Colourful, yes, but very phoney. Pseudo," he mumbled. "But the food here always used to be very good."

I did not care. To my inexperienced eyes – I think to

Dick's as well – it was simply exciting.

We were directed to a screened alcove, asked about drinks, and then the menu was brought.

"I don't know any of this," I said to Donald. "And I don't think Dick knows very much." I turned to him.

"No," Dick answered. "Please, Donald, you order. We are in your hands."

And our Major reeled off the meal he wanted for the three of us, in Urdu. The headwaiter listened politely, smiled and explained in perfect English: "Sir, you are only allowed one main dish, that is the law."

The civilian Ferguson gave way to the military Ferguson with a burst of temper. He again spoke in Urdu, and the waiter stiffened, bowed and went away. Dick clarified the situation, spoke about food rationing and generally tried to calm him down. He was still angry, hurt, that a soldier who has come home at last, is subject to restrictions which, in his mind, ought to have disappeared by the end of the war.

After a while a team of waiters appeared with a large assortment of dishes. Surely, this must be far more than the usual allocation? All due to Urdu? A smiling Donald rewarded the headwaiter with a generous tip and yet another flood of this strange language. All was well; we enjoyed a superb meal and had altogether a most interesting evening.

Somehow, this strange crude man touches me, and we can really know only the people and things that touch us. Everything else is like words from a dictionary: we can learn them, but do we understand them? They do not live deep inside us. This man makes me curious. I want to know more about him, want to probe. He does not let me. He left as he arrived.

"We'll keep in touch," he said, and "I am glad to see you settled happily and with so much confidence." The shoes, I wonder?

"I'll see you again, I hope. And thanks. Thanks a lot."

We haven't heard from him yet.

11 April 1951

We all should take life as it comes, and deal with it. It is no good dreaming of what it ought to be. We crumble when things go against us, but picking ourselves up, not being daunted, that – in the end – is the saving grace.

I have to do just that, but it is incredibly hard sometimes. I discover my real strength only when matters go badly, and then it is no good bottling feelings up, leaving them to rot. It is so much better to talk, even if afterwards I have to cry alone.

My husband, however, does not want to talk about Roy. To him, the decision made was right and a very good one for the boy. He thinks I am selfish and sorry for myself. On this particular occasion he does only want to talk about one thing: Canada. There is a good position waiting for him near Toronto, he is very enthusiastic. He seems to expect quite naturally that I would share his pleasure in the offer. That I would uproot myself once more, without question this time. That I would readily give up our home, and my newly acquired friends, after not yet four years in England. Is his work so all-consuming for him? Or is he, deep down and secretly, restless because Roy has left? Either way, the answer has to be 'no'. If only he would show exasperation sometimes with my 'erratic' behaviour (his expression) or my tears. But he is simply kind, watches me and never tries to break through my obstinacy.

After we talked, he simply said, "Come, let's go for a walk."

Silence for a long time, and then finally: "I am going. I want to go. I feel so restless. I know I can do better than here."

'Better than here.' He thinks of money. Hardly of money for himself though, I know that. But I am not interested. In the past, I had to live on so very little. Money does not matter. Belonging does. And his ideas deeply upset my sense of belonging and the joyous feeling of being safe.

"It is a challenge," he said. "I want to try. If you do not want to go with me, give me six months, a year perhaps. Nothing lost. I know my firm here will take me back."

I choked a little. "Find out, but leave me here, for the time being anyway. I belong here now, don't take me away."

His sense of responsibility is very strong: "Go on living here as if I were with you. I'll look after you as far as money is concerned. Go to Germany for a while. Start looking for an interesting new job. We'll talk again. Give me some time."

His work might not be of terrific importance to anybody else, but it is vital to him. It allows him to be the way he is. Nobody has the right to change that. "Yes," I say to myself, "we have to be the way we are. If we try to be different, something eventually will have to give. It is like putting our feet into the wrong shoes; we end up feeling very uncomfortable. And, in any case, do we not have to accept that the only thing which is permanent is change?"

What clever theories I am developing now! Although none of them is of great comfort at present.

A week ago I broke my handmirror. I know I am stupid. It cannot possibly make the slightest difference to any future event. My reason tells me plainly that breaking a mirror is no more than a bore. Just the same, I have been miserable with the suspicion ever since. Now I know the reason.

30 May 1951

It is a beautiful spring day. I went to Southampton with Dick. He was looking forward to the voyage. He has time for a leisurely boat trip. First New York, then on to

Toronto. New York! Of course I want to visit it as well, of course I want to be with him. Why have I made such a silly decision? I simply do not know at this moment. Only that I do not want to leave my newly-found country again so soon.

He was excited, already away from his home and me. I felt desperately lonely when the gang planks were removed, lines cast off, the ship's siren sounded and when, finally, she pulled slowly away from the quay. People were leaning over the side, waving, throwing streamers. I stood on the stone pier and stared in awe at the ship. Vast, mountainous, dazzling white, festooned with flags, crowded with passengers. How does it stay afloat? It is so huge. In spite of my misery, I had to laugh at myself. Dick, had he been by my side, would have laughed as well. I am so incredibly ignorant of scientific matters, and we both know it. I waved too, but I did not see him, my eyes were blind with tears. What now? I walked back into town, a long walk. I did not want to gaze out across the water, it was better to look at the scars of war the town still showed. It suited my mood. A slight haze covered the sun, a warm breeze blew up from the harbour. It is a spring of golden abundance, and I shall have to celebrate it alone now.

How strange it is to return to an empty house and to know I shall be alone there for months to come. Nobody now to worry if I am late coming home. Nobody to cosset me if I am not well, and nobody to laugh with me, or offer reassurance when I need it. It hurts, but it is impossible to push such thoughts into the background. It is a little like an aching tooth: one keeps on probing if the pain is actually still there. It nearly always is. And the cruel iciness of lonely war years begins to trickle through my body. I shall not allow it to. I open the French windows to the warm night and black Caesar, the cat, comes in, purring and wrapping herself round my legs. I pick her up and sit down in my favourite armchair. I look at my wedding ring and have to smile: it is not my wedding ring at all. It is my mother-in-law's, and she gave it to Dick when he told her we were going to be married. In those days, it was not easy to buy a golden ring.

Dick's mother had been a widow for a long time and told him that 'the engagement ring she wore would be all she needed.' I had not had an engagement ring either. Not that I missed it: the custom was unknown in Germany then. On a promise of marriage the bride-to-be received her wedding ring from her fiancé and wore it on her left hand until the marriage ceremony, during which it was transferred to the right hand. The same applied to the groom.

There is a love that begins in the head and goes down to the heart and grows, very slowly, but it lasts. It is not a series of sensations, it is different: growing affection, friendship, even a sense of loss sometimes. I mean to say that our love was not a mutual 'this is it' explosion, but grew out of compassion, respect for one another's lonely past and, on both sides, curiosity on a large scale: Will you be understanding? Will you tolerate ideas that may be alien to you? Will you be able to love me in spite of what I am? Perhaps on the surface this is rather a cool assessment of individual points but, underlying, there is a great warm feeling of trust.

It is well past midnight. I have been sitting here all the time, with the cat still on my lap. I have to face up to reality once more, rather than having someone else doing it for me. He had made a decision, he wanted to go. I am far less apprehensive now and, in any case, I am blessed with natural optimism. I do not want to be uprooted, so, I have to start again, on my own for a while. A new day brings new tasks, new pleasure perhaps. Do I sound like Scarlet O'Hara? 'Tomorrow is another day . . .'

1 June 1951

The morning began with a great sense of joy: a big bunch of flowers arrived. 'I love you', the card said, 'be patient with me. I know it's going to be alright.'

Yes, of course it will be. But what about now? I do not want to work as a translator again, always on my own. I want people around me. I long to teach German, but there are still not many chances. Germany? Yes, when summer comes. It will be good to see my family, particularly as I am going there alone. Maybe there will be less friction then, and I will not have to watch anxiously all the time if Dick is treated kindly and with tolerance. It will be good, too, to visit our old friends

Gisela and Helmut. And part of Henning's school holidays could definitely be spent with him. Perhaps I would get permission to revisit Stettin, my home town? All this will mean a few weeks of distraction, of getting over the loneliness that lurks in the back of my mind.

I plan a visit for July and will write to my parents about it. In my letter I'll also ask them to organise Henning's stay in Kiel for the same time. Then I'll apply at the Polish Embassy in London for a visa to visit Stettin. I feel good as I always do when I am actually doing something constructive. There will be more work in the house for me now. We had seen to many of the daily, recurring tasks together. He is very untidy, though. What kind of life will it be if I cannot grumble about a special kitchen knife that has wandered into the garage, burnt potatoes (if he decided to cook), splashes of paint on doors or pieces of furniture after a room has been beautifully decorated, or forgotten phone messages? How will I cope without him, even if he has his shortcomings? And the garden! It has become an important part of our lives. A few years ago I had to learn very much, when I came to own the first garden in my life. And I am still learning, but now without a man in the house. House and garden are like Tower Bridge: one unending maintenance job. Stop doing things to the house – or the garden, for that matter – they turn round and do nasty things to you. All I hope for is that Dick will be back before the house turns against me.

5 June 1951

As so often in my life, exactly the right thing happens at exactly the right time: A note through the letter box asking for people interested in amateur dramatics. A well established Ilford group needs new blood. How would I fit in? Would I be able to learn English lines? Would the group accept me? Even if only for back stage help? I feel sufficiently confident, although Dick is not here to support me, to make a telephone call to the producer who had signed the leaflet.

"You have an attractive voice," he said, "there is an accent. Where do you come from?"

This is it once more.

"You may not like it," I answered. "Germany."

He laughed. "Why shouldn't I? Come along on Thursday night, eight o'clock. We are in the small room in the library. Let's have a look at each other."

And I think again, as so often in the past, how easy it appears to be. I hope I can really do something with these people. I need an absorbing leisure pursuit more than ever before, and I know I can act. But in English?

7 June 1951

I have just received a very friendly, welcoming letter from my parents. Henning also wrote to say that he will be in Kiel from mid-July. Only the Polish Embassy cannot make up their minds about allowing me to visit my home town. I wonder how long we will have to wait before we are allowed there again.

8 June 1951

Rehearsal night came and I had to face about twenty people, male and female, young and not so young. The producer stepped forward and introduced me to everyone. "I think she may be what we need for all the foreign maids', wives' and way-out diplomats' parts." He went on to ask me whether I had acted before, or whether I can speak French and other details.

He has quite an abrupt way of talking. Fast, too. I had to listen very carefully. He is unquestionably the dominant figure amongst all of them. Tall and lean, tanned, and with the eyes of a man who has spent a long time in the sun. Or at sea? Silver-grey hair, brushed back. When I spoke to him on the phone I had visualized a much younger man.

I explained that my French is fine, but not, perhaps, for the stage. But he said it was alright. They want to put on 'Quiet Wedding' in the second week of July. I do not know the play, but had a look at the script there. It is a comedy.

July? I did some quick thinking – Kiel, Henning . . . I might have to change the July dates a little, that is, if I am accepted.

We all read the script. Not everyone knew the play. I was very nervous when we started reading, and only lost the tense 'new girl' feeling when my Mme Mirelle, a French dressmaker who has to try out a bridesmaid's dress on a young girl, complains in exasperation: "C'est impossible, zees vooly vest undernees. She must take off al her clos or I cannot fit ze dress properly. Mon Dieu! Ze figures of ze young English!" And they laughed, they actually laughed. I felt happy and relaxed. Perhaps I will get this part. It is not a big role, which suits me.

I have never, since my school days, had to learn English verse or prose and, apart from Robert Browning's 'Oh, to be in England' and one or two monologues from Shakespeare's historic plays I can only recite nursery rhymes I have learned from Roy when I first looked after him. My mind started wandering: How is he? His last letter came in time for Christmas. And Henning? And Dick? I forgot the group around me and sank back into my very own sadness.

"Hey Pat, where are you? Don't you like it? Come on, let's try Act Three."

"Oh, yes, of course I like it. Which page?"

I took a deep breath. Here was a marvellous chance to fill my loneliness. How silly to dwell on problems I have – in part anyway – created for myself. I looked at the text, page eighty, listened and pushed everything else out of my mind.

9 June 1951

Charles, the producer, rang to tell me that I am the right French dressmaker for the play. Now I'll have to rehearse with the 'Ilford Players' twice, sometimes three times, a week. I am looking forward to evenings of work, talk and drink in good company. In that order.

How strange it is that each defined period of our lives is woven into a pattern, but it is not always possible to pick up the right thread at the moment we need it most. This time, however, it was. I am very fortunate indeed.

25 June 1951

Dick writes often. I am always eagerly awaiting his mail. He is a good letter-writer and describes in great detail, and often in a very amusing way, how he tries to adjust to his new colleagues, how he runs his small household and how he spends his weekends. He talks of Leamington, Stratford, Windsor, – names so familiar yet over three thousand miles away. It seems odd to me: We live in Essex and Windsor in Canada is in the County of Essex as well. It makes me feel a little nearer to him. I envy him the weekends. Mine are usually very quietly spent in the garden, sometimes with Dick's mother, and now and again in Walton with Aunt Rose and the cousins. He goes to the Great Lakes, to Detroit through the Windsor-Detroit tunnel, one of the biggest engineering achievements in the world, I learn, or to Stratford to see a Shakespeare play. Oh, why had I stayed at home? For the hundredth time I ask myself the old question, but now I refuse to analyse and brood over it. It is high time to put an end to my doubts, to prepare for events to come: the play, the trip to Germany and a holiday with Henning. There is something else, very exciting for me, which could mean a breakthrough after years of friction between Marianne, my sister, and myself. She has asked if she could visit me, perhaps travelling with me on my return to England.

"I'll never do it alone," she had written, "and I feel I ought to see how you live now. I don't think I'll like it, but I don't want to be prejudiced any longer either. So, the only solution is to come and see for myself. I have never forgotten how close we were in the war years, although I do not believe we can recapture that ever."

She is probably right, but the fact that she has written to me in this manner, not just a perfunctory note added to my mother's or father's letters and that she actually wanted to see England, is marvellous news.

After weeks of waiting, the Polish Embassy has sent a questionnaire and has expressed doubts about a visit to Stettin. Why do I want to go there? I was born there, but I am the holder of a British Passport. Those two do not go together. Am I going to spy? For the British? For the West-Germans? It is all very complicated and, in the end, when I explained that I only want to see my home town again, they refused. Perhaps it is just as well. The town would not be the same. 85% of it has been destroyed. Everything would look different and would not waken memories. Better so. Why open up old wounds? I know from German newspapers I occasionally receive that there are, of the 300,000 inhabitants of Stettin who had survived the war, only 2,000 who were allowed to stay, mainly working in the Polish docks or being employed in the fishing industry. I read that they work without pay, and the black market is rampant. Building materials from ruins are transported to Warsaw, German cemeteries are ploughed up and the gravestones sold. No, I do not want the picture I have of my birthplace and my young years there destroyed. Goodbye, Stettin.

I booked a ticket: Liverpool Street, Harwich – Hoek van Holland – Hamburg – Kiel. A long trip! From six o'clock in the evening to mid-afternoon the next day. My first return to Germany in 1949 had – unlike this one – been very carefree. Dick had been with me. This time I have to find my own way. As always, without him I feel apprehensive.

9 July 1951

In the afternoon, before the first performance of 'Quiet Wedding', Dick rang.

"Hello, Pat. This is just to say toi toi toi and break your

neck and leg."

"What? How do you know that saying?"

"Well, that's what your people wish actors before the opening of a play, isn't it?"

"Yes, it is. But it sounds awful in English."

"I know. A German here told me, it is their way to wish somebody luck." Then a long pause and "I wish I could be there. Don't become too ambitious. Don't forget I need you more than your new friends do."

Does he remember what I had told him about the acting ambitions of my youth? He need not fear anything. This is just going to be a pastime, fun.

And yet, when the evening came, I was not only nervous, but very frightened. Would I be good enough? Would I perhaps let the team down? The people I came to like very much, who welcomed me without many questions? Rubbish! It is only a small part anyway, and I can and will do it. Standing in the wings, waiting for my first entrance, I sensed the audience. They were all out there, waiting. All eighty of them! I swore not a word would come out when I opened my mouth. Everybody round me could hear my heart beating, I was sure. Now. I opened the door to make that entrance. Thank goodness, it was alright. The handle did not come off as it did yesterday during dress rehearsal. And I could hear my own voice, loud and clear. Suddenly the joy of acting took over, everything else forgotten. Some of the audience laughed. How that helped!

I invited the cast all back to our house. Would Dick have liked that? They are so easy going, open in their opinions, arguing in the friendliest way, laughing a lot. I wonder. He would probably be sitting in a corner, watching, but always ready to help with drinks, sandwiches and the never-ending pot of coffee. He is such a serious man, attentive but hesitant to join in.

15 July 1951

My neighbour called. She is a widow, quite old but very lively and helpful.

"Hello, Pat. Would you like to come with me to a church bazaar on Saturday morning? Have you ever been to one?"

"No, I am sorry. We are not churchgoers." I felt embarrassed.

"That does not matter in the least," she assured me. "Come, you'll enjoy it. They are holding a 'bring and buy' sale as well."

Bring and buy? So I take something I do not want, donate it and buy one or two items? What a strange idea!

"You can pick up all sorts of useful things for pennies. It's amazing how much money comes together on these occasions."

The purpose in this case is, I hear, to provide money

for repairing the roof of our local church. Ah well, I do not like to say 'no' and accompany her to the church hall. Cake and bottle stalls, stands with home-made jam, tomato chutney and plants catch my eye as well as a few stalls enjoyed by youngsters particularly, where they can have a lucky dip or buy toys, books or games for very little money. And then there is the 'White Elephant Stall'. What on earth is that? When I look at it closely I come to the conclusion that it contains all the presents one was given at one time, but never wanted: mirrors in hideous frames, lace handkerchiefs in pretty boxes, talcum powder not showing the favourite make, numerous small dishes and ashtrays inscribed 'souvenir' from Margate, Clacton or Blackpool, mingling with some lovely Victoriana. This, as bazaars go, might have been worse, and I thank my neighbour for taking me. I return home with some jam, two beautiful old salt and pepper pots and a couple of plants.

I have never known anything like it in Germany. What a clever idea to raise money for a good cause! Nobody has to pay out much. You spend your pennies having some pleasure in the company of like-minded people, you can listen to a school band at the same time, enjoy the inevitable cup of tea served by cheerful members of the church and, above all, wallow in the feeling you have done your good deed for the day. Voluntary aid and charity are two clearly defined terms which, in the English language, ought to be written in capital letters. I like it.

How different this is from a Nazi warden appearing

on our doorstep every Sunday morning, asking for a donation towards 'winter aid' which, as the war went on, became a permanent demand, all the year round. We never dared to refuse money and were always told to eat a simple vegetable casserole instead of a Sunday joint. As if a good roast still existed! In this manner we would not miss the money. We all were very sure that the funds thus collected nationwide went into the Nazi Party coffers, but hardly anybody ever spoke his mind. It was too dangerous.

Walton *Saturday 21 July 1951*

End of July, and I have started preparing for my visit to Germany. Why is it that I suddenly feel so listless? Of course I want to see my family, Henning above all. Why is it so hard to think of presents, packing, getting the house in order? The aftermath of the play which leaves me with a peculiarly flat feeling? Worry about Dick? No need for that, I tell myself. I try to fight off the vague, uncertain sensation that holds me back and, instead, force myself to look ahead.

This is the last weekend before I am due to set off, so I came to old Walton. Two days with Dick's aunt. Only I do not spend much time with her. I am drawn to the water. I love the sea, love listening to the roll and crash of the waves, to the surf. At present it is a vast shimmering sheet of silver, and above it the hazy blue sky is piled high with luminous clouds. The sea is like a human being, always moving, always something deep inside it stirring. It never rests. And then, when it cannot reach what it wants, it creeps slowly back, disappointed, moaning sometimes. It always asks questions, it never gets or gives an answer. I lie down on the sands, watch the tide coming in and with it the great breakers, and listen to the mournful sound of the seagulls. Do they say what I feel? Endless search, endless longing. I do not know myself for what.

I think back, picturing the Baltic coast of my childhood days: the gently curved bays with thatched cottages, the smell of moss and huge pines, the silvery beaches only washed by the sea when there are violent gales. Of course there are forests here, but they smell differently. The sense of smell brings back childhood memories very strongly. Perhaps as a child we are closer to the soil, the earth?

On the boat to Hoek-van-Holland. *25 July 1951*

Joyce and Roy have taken me to Liverpool Street Station.

"Don't," I argued, "I can find my own way."

"Nonsense," Roy said, "what are friends for?" And: "You will come back, won't you?" (Do I detect some anxiety?) "We'll be here again on the 25th August. You gave us the time of the train."

"Yes, thank you. And don't forget I'll come back with my sister and Maria. We'll go and visit her parents near Krefeld, then travel together."

They kissed me goodbye. I love them for it whereas, only four years ago, I had resented the ease with which people kiss each other, even if only on the cheeks. I had never been used to it. 'Just like the Russians' I thought then. But no longer. It means warmth and affection now.

Kiel *August 1951*

Seeing Henning again always fills me with so much happiness that I do not feel like doing anything else. Perhaps it is to him I have been writing all these years. To tell him everything that I would like to tell but could not, he being so far away, so protected from me. But when I see him I know that he is and will always be my little boy. So big now – he is 12! I know I still cannot take him back with me to England, but each day that passes I feel more secure, assured that one day he will be able to come and stay with us. For the time being I don't want to think about it.

The rest of my so-called homecoming has been disappointing and depressing. Mother is ill, very ill, I believe. "Is it cancer?" I asked Marianne. "Nobody will admit it," was her answer. Meanwhile doctors continue with tests all the time. Mother looks so tired and weak.

She was gentle and friendly, when I saw her this time, similar to last year, when I first discovered her to be softer, showing me that she cared about me and even Dick. "Talk to me about your life over there," she would say, but did not really listen. And she could not bear boisterous Henning around her for long periods. I had to shield her from his noisy presence and go out with him fishing, sailing with Helmut, visiting a cinema or a maritime museum, having endless ice creams and beautiful German cakes with whipped cream on top. He is twelve years old now, very intelligent and full of questions about practically everything. It was such a joy to be with him and I wanted to cling, to take him with me to ask again why I had to give him up. Deep down I know, of course, that such feelings are futile.

Kiel *18 August 1951*

Kiel has put on weight since the war, is nourished with overemployment and fat contracts. It is burping with prosperity, gleaming with new buildings and roads and wearing a halo of righteousness and hard work. Never before in German history, I think, has there been such a universal passion for private gain. From the void of a phoney, overheated idealism the Germans have plunged into work and materialism. Workers compete for overtime, their wives for factory or office jobs, and when the children come home from school, which finishes at lunch time, they are kept in an illusory kind of order by grandmothers or old neighbours. Or, worse, they become 'key-children', wearing the key for their flat on a chain or cord around their neck. They are on their own and it is not suprising that during their games in gravel pits and on building sites gangs are being formed that begin with petty pilfering and develop, to bring off one coup after another. At the expense of their hardworking, money-grubbing elders. A homeless generation is growing up, floundering in unstable times and playing at crime.

Walking along watching a group of children close by, and thinking about the strange aggression and apparent independence they show, I am suddenly stopped by a little girl. She comes running up to me, curtsies politely and says in a timid, quiet voice: "I think this is yours. You dropped it." She smiles and holds up a handkerchief.

"Thank you." I cannot say any more. In England you only curtsy to the King or Queen. How is it possible that I see a nice little girl, belonging to a rough gang of children and yet, she is so friendly and polite. Perhaps I am wrong about it all?

My thoughts go back to Frau Wolf, the first German to stay with us when I myself was relatively new in England. She is a civil servant in Rendsburg now, not very far away from Kiel. Christmas cards are exchanged regularly, but are still – according to her wish – very formal greetings. Perhaps she would like to see me? Perhaps we could meet? I ring her at her office in the town hall, she sounds delighted.

"How are you?" And she continues in very good English, but it is all a little stilted. She does not want to speak of herself, so I cannot probe or touch on emotional involvement, and it develops into everyday small talk, which, quite generally, it often does on the telephone. In any case, it is very difficult to express personal feelings in a foreign language. By the same token, it is easy to swear in an acquired tongue. It never seems quite as strong and bad as in one's own. I learned to use 'damn' in a very casual way, whereas I would hardly ever have said 'verdammt' in German.

I understand the desire of the Germans to live in the present. Perhaps they provide a lesson English people could learn from. The English do not live enough in it. Many people in England sneer at the German obsession with material wealth, but if they had lost as much as their opponent, money, at least, is a tangible reality. Aren't we, in fact, just as preoccupied with it as they are, without doing as much to make it fructify? We make such heavy weather about mobility of labour: should we not admire how they, in the midst of massive reconstruction, rehabilitate millions of their fellow-countrymen who are refugees? Should all Germans walk around, downcast by a collective feeling of guilt? And keep very quiet not to draw anyone's attention? Unthinkable in Germany. There is boisterous, carefree life, laughter, noise, a lot of it.

Just the same, I see many grey faces, fear and suspicion in the eyes of older people. There had been three types of Germans, when I belonged there, generally speaking: Convinced, passionate Nazis (but there were relatively few of them), a very large number of opportunists who often joined the Nazi Party thinking of their own advantages and possible safety and those, who never were Party members. Some of them worked actively against the ruling system. But, I think, it cannot do any good now to search around with a divining rod trying to find the guilty ones.

I tear up the picture of these recent impressions and memories and decide: 'The German file is closed'. Why then do I at times feel haunted by a past life that follows on my heels everywhere and which I cannot shake off? I feel very sad and frustrated, both at my inability to change things and my refusal to accept them as they are.

On the boat back to Hoek-van-Holland 25 August 1951

The sea is glittering in the heat of the August day. I feel hot, restless, uneasy. The sadness I know so well filling heart and mind every time I leave Henning behind, simply will not go away. And why this uneasiness? In part because Marianne is on the boat as well, excited about her first visit to England but, as always, very critical of the people around her and, as many of the passengers are British, she has much to comment on. How would she react to Dick's family, our friends and the house?

But that is not all: I feel physically restless, though without my 'proverbial' (according to Dick) energy. Perhaps I ought to see old Dr Mcdonald, our family doctor. We have not needed him very often, but he is good to talk to and always has plenty of time for his patients. He is a neighbour of ours as well.

Marianne and Maria joined me on deck. My sister and I had broken our journey to stop with Maria's family in a little village not far from Krefeld in the Ruhr area of Germany, and then continued our return to England together with her. Marianne likes Maria and, in a way, travelling with her has made the relationship between us a little easier.

"Look," I said, "you can just see the coast line." We strained our eyes against the bright sunlight, and then Marianne asked:

"But where are the famous white cliffs? This is all flat and rather grey."

"The white cliffs of Dover are much further south," I laughed. "This is the Essex coast, a little like the North Sea shore in Schleswig-Holstein."

I should not have laughed. She does not like to be corrected. I have to be more careful.

Not much longer to go. In a short while we are going to dock in Harwich harbour. Once more that familiar pain makes itself noted: my heart yearning for Henning, my reasoning and my love for Dick drawing me towards England. An old sailor joined us at the railing and started chatting. I looked at him. He must have been across the Channel and the North Sea countless times, and he too must know something about having roots in more than one country.

Home *26 August 1951*

Arriving in Harwich yesterday, Marianne and I did not have much luggage, but Maria dragged three enormous suitcases along. She has parents who will sacrifice anything they possibly can to make her new life more comfortable. When I asked her: "What on earth is in those cases?" she replied:

"Oh, bed linen, towels and things, household bits, anything they (her family) can spare." Lucky Maria!

The customs officer asked her to open the cases.

"I open this one," she said, 'the other two are just feather beds."She pronounced it 'fesser beds' and meant eiderdowns.

"I beg your pardon?" The officer was not unfriendly, but definitely puzzled.

"Fesser beds, you know, for sleeping."

"Please, open all of them." He was quite firm.

"I warn you!" Maria tried hard. "*You* will have to shut them again."

He looked confused, but insisted. "Never mind," he said.

He opened the first one and found nothing interesting, then turned his attention to the other two. As he released the catches, the lids of the suitcases burst open and the 'fesser beds' billowed forth. He then saw his problem: the very voluminous German eiderdowns her parents had given her to replace the English style blankets she could not get used to.

"So," Maria said with a charming smile and in a very determined voice. "Now you shut them again. You have to sit on them, you know. I warned you, didn't I?"

I like her. And how I envy her the fluffy continental eider-downs, practically unheard of in England, despised by Dick because he has never been used to them, for ever leaving me struggling with sheets, blankets, 'tucking in' methods. Oh, for a soft, cuddly 'fesser bed'!

29 August 1951

Breakfast time, mail, the newspaper. I love that time of the morning. A big pot of good strong coffee, toast and marmalade, the sun shining into the dining room, what could be better? Even Marianne likes it and seems relaxed.

But this morning everything was wrong. I received a letter from Henning: "Please do not write to my home any longer. I'll give you the name and address of a friend of mine. A really good one. Do you remember? I told you about Heinz. His father has a boat and we go fishing together. There is always trouble when I have spent time with you."

I am shocked. What shall I do? I cannot encourage him to have secrets from his father. He is only twelve years old. He is obviously torn by divided loyalties. Should I tell Marianne? No, not just now. I think I must write to Klaus and plead to let him live with us. After all, he has a small daughter now and, I hear, has found happiness. There has been official recognition of West-Germany since 1949, and we would have the right to bring Henning up in this country. I do not have to ask Dick about this at all. He would be utterly supportive, I know. Thinking back to Kiel, the boy had appeared more disturbed than he normally was when we had to part.

I decided to write to Klaus. It is the first time in all these years that I wrote to Henning's father. I did it very gently, carefully. In the meantime, I shall not write to my son. Klaus has to see my reasoning, has to acknowledge that the boy longs to be with his mother.

5 September 1951

That was wishful thinking. Klaus' reply came quite quickly. Not from him exactly, but from a solicitor:

> "While Herr Dr Schwarz is extremely grateful for your honest approach he, at the same time, wishes to express that he does not desire any interference in his son's upbringing. The boy has been told to stop sending you another address. Naturally, there is no hindering your correspondence. However, once and for all: until he is of age, Henning will live and be educated in Germany."

I am shattered, cry, feel numbed. That is the reward for my heartfelt plea? How he must hate me! Perhaps there is an even stronger emotion than that: racial hatred. He is, after all, an old disciple of National Socialism. I cannot believe any of it. Marianne again. Should I show her this letter? I do not think so. Our fragile relationship would be totally destroyed if I have to face the fact that she sides with Klaus.

6 September 1951

I have made an appointment to see the doctor tomorrow. According to Marianne, I should have done it long ago, for 'I have been very difficult and touchy most of the time'. I said nothing. Of course I am touchy and feel vulnerable after Klaus' letter. Besides, there is hardly anything Marianne approves of in my household. Nor does she like the friends I introduce her to. 'Too informal' is her verdict.

We have been everywhere: the Tower, for walks along the Embankment, an area I particularly love. My favourite stroll, with Big Ben standing proud and tall beside the Houses of Parliament, watching couples walking along, arms twined around each others' waist, on a summer evening. How I long for Dick! We took a boat down the Thames to Greenwich one day. We wandered around the big stores where she is constantly surprised and amused that you can try hats on without anybody pressing you into buying.

She is right there. I remember my own reluctance when entering a shop in Germany in the past, being absolutely certain that I would immediately be bombarded by shop assistants who were often too servile in their initial attitude towards potential customers, but reverted to arrogance when I failed to purchase something. In contrast, here I can look and rummage to my heart's content without being pestered. It is as if sales people have no great interest in you buying anything and, considering their easy-going way, I wonder occasionally how England won the war. Perhaps these thoughts are in Marianne's mind too? And become the source of her utter disbelief? I shall not ask her. It might lead to further arguments. Whatever I show her: the Palace, parks, churches, her standard reaction is always the same. "They are very lucky that we did not destroy more of this town." I feel hurt and really do not know what else I can offer to please her.

Yet this is only part of my concern. Why am I so listless? So vaguely discontented, even melancholy at times? Marianne is not the cause for that. Dick writes regularly, telephones quite often late at night, I have no financial worries. The answer, I feel sure, is a talk with our nice Scottish doctor. He is a good listener. Patient with children, too. A few times in the past I had to take Roy to see him.

A VERY IMPORTANT DAY *7 September 1951*

Sitting in the waiting room, I was again amazed at the general shabbiness and lack of care in an English family doctor's surgery. No young, often glamorous receptionist in a white coat, no door marked 'laboratory'. A simple waiting room, reminiscent of a rather run-down lounge in a private house, lots of old magazines – were all suburban surgeries like this? A German medical practitioner shows in every manner what an important professional man he is: well dressed, white-coated, his consulting room gleaming, smelling of disinfectant, all sorts of gadgets and apparatus spread around. Everything rather awe-inspiring, putting you in your place. Yes, this is different, in a way comforting, familiar. I did not really know what to tell him. It would all sound a little muddled, indistinct, probably uninteresting to an experienced,well-established doctor.

A few minutes later I realised how wrong I was. He listened carefully, then took my blood pressure, looked at my fingernails, eyes, throat, and nearly made me fall off the chair I was sitting in, when he finally asked: "When did you last have a period?"

Of course! I had not thought of that at all, had dismissed any irregularity lightly, worrying about Dick, living alone, going to Germany which always means a slight change of climate and food. Those, I thought, were the reasons for any change in the routine.

I gasped: "Do you think I am pregnant?"

"I don't know," was his reply. "Let's find out."

And a little later: "You told me your husband is abroad, didn't you? Well, you'd better get him back later in the year, you might need him."

He beamed at me, his bright blue eyes twinkling in the big, ruddy face.

"Good luck, everything seems perfect. See me again in eight weeks time."

Just like that. So easy, so casual, and yet so reassuring.

I went home in a daze. At the end of a hot September day there was a fine mist around me, making everything very soft-edged and beautiful, a little unreal, as I slowly approached our house, walking through the local park. Unreal? But this is real. I am going to have a baby. I have often thought of myself as of somebody to whom things happen rather than a person who causes events. This, however, I would make happen: a child for Dick and me. I would finally have roots again, through our baby. England would truly be my country then. I smiled to myself in the comfortable glow of a deep, warm feeling. The end of one life, the beginning of another.

Someone passed me: "Hello, Pat, how are you?" Our neighbour's daughter. I felt at home.

"What did the doctor say?" Marianne looked at me. "You look different. What's the matter? Did he give you a tonic?"

"Oh yes, he did. Everything will be fine. I'm a little run down." I found it impossible to tell her about my pregnancy. Later perhaps. I am afraid she could say something cynical and upset my happiness.

16 September 1951

The last week of Marianne's stay has been peaceful. She cannot do anything any longer to upset me. I have kept my secret. I have even kept it from Dick. Only for a little while longer, I tell myself and, at the same time, look forward to talking to him, sensing his reaction over the telephone. Any day now, but first Marianne has to go back to Germany. I want to be alone with him when I let him know. After that, I shall write to my family.

There is a certain feeling of guilt, though, as I waved goodbye to my sister at Liverpool Street Station. Suddenly, she no longer looked hard, forbidding even, but sad and lonely. She is going back to our parents and her son, but not to a home of her own and a loving husband. How lucky I am.

17 September 1951

I rang Dick today.

"Hello, Pat, how are things?" Down to earth, flat voice, no sign of pleasure that I called him. How well I know it!

"Fine. What about you?"

"Ah, I am very pleased with myself. The firm is sending me to Ottawa for the next two months. Should be interesting. A good step forward too. I've written to you in detail about this. Are you impressed?"

"Very," I laughed. "Good luck to you. Does that mean you'll stay longer than planned?"

"What did we plan," he replied. "If I want to, I can stay here for a long time. But you know, I'll only do that if you join me, if you change your mind."

Here goes. I took a deep breath.

"I would like you to be home for Christmas." I must have sounded very timid.

"You try to keep me away. I have already arranged for three weeks holiday."

"No, I don't mean just for Christmas. I want to say, you should be here from Christmas on."

A long pause.

"Pat? What's wrong? Are you ill?" All of a sudden the voice was no longer flat but anxious, caring.

"No, dear. But I think I need a man about the house, all through January. We are going to have a baby."

"We what?" He shouted into the telphone, and after that there was a long silence three thousand miles away. Then a pleading, hurried – "Please, say it again. Did you say, a baby?"

"Yes, I did, darling. At last! Are you happy?"

"Happy?" Now there was panic in his voice. "Yes, yes, I am happy. I'll cancel Ottawa, I'll cancel everything. I'm coming home straightaway."

"No, you are not." I tried to calm his excitement. "Come home towards the end of the year. I am perfectly well and, for once, *I* am thinking of money."

We argued a little, and I was touched by the concern this quiet, reserved man of mine could convey across the Atlantic, through soulless telephone cables.

I put the receiver down, went into the lounge and searched amongst records. *Beethoven's Pastorale.* Yes, that was right for my present mood: serene music, harmonious. I leaned back in my favourite armchair and let the waves of sound envelop me.

3rd November 1951

I wonder: should I buy a piano before Dick comes home? The money is there. He looks after me extremely well. But, would he agree? He likes Fats Waller and Duke Ellington, but I am not that type of player. I cannot play boogie-woogie either, his kind of rhythm. And, he would hardly enjoy my classical and romantic piano music. Still, the instrument could stand in the dining room, it would not disturb him too much then. He might even acquire a taste for an entirely different type of music. After all, I like jazz – a bit.

Should I ask him when he next rings? No. I am going to surprise him, hoping he will not resent the money being spent on my pleasure alone. We need extra money for the baby. I am aware of that, but Canada has been very good for our financial situation, and I feel certain he would willingly let me have my way. We have talked about it in the past.

20 November 1951

I went out today and bought a reconditioned 'Berry' piano with a beautiful, rich tone. Mahogany too! That, at least should please Dick and his way of seeing the practical side of everything. I have that wonderful sense of achievement now.

Any day now Dick will be home, and I am ready for him. I do not want to do any housework during the first days with him. I want hours to listen and to talk, look at photos and enjoy the company of 'my man' in our home.

What a strange thing memory is! I remember certain unimportant happenings in our life together and forget important ones. I have to close my eyes and think hard to remember his serious face. Some events register in detail, others appear behind a veil of mist. And the more I try to concentrate, the further away reality slips. Like dreams: I wake up in the morning and remember a dream vividly. A few seconds later it has disappeared and leaves a strange, sad void.

I look into the mirror. Will he still like me? Short hair now, cut to a shiny cap, light brown as always. What will he think of it? He used to love my long hair. Grey-blue eyes, the same high cheekbones, a wide mouth, square, very white teeth, no make-up. I do not like it at all for myself. Perhaps a leftover from the Hitler years: 'The German woman does not smoke and she does not wear make-up.' How well I remember the posters!

I sigh a little: that's who I am. He'd better put up with me again. After all, marriage is a never-ending series of emotional adjustments. It requires determination, watchfulness,and a capacity for loving. All of this we find in family life. The family – that is truly all there ever is. And we would have our own English family soon.

23 November 1951

I am waiting for Dick's telephone call from Southampton. There will be plenty of time then to go to Liverpool Street Station and meet him. With flowers, of course, as we used to do in Germany. It ought to be today, and I dare not leave the house in case I miss his call. I am listening to "Mrs Dale's Diary", a radio programme I have become very fond of. The doorbell is ringing.

It was him!

There he stood at the door, with suitcases, a bag and a big bunch of red roses. He came by taxi. So much for my plans!

For a second we did not say anything, but there was immediate contact.

"It's good to be home." We embraced. "Gosh! How big you are!"

"And proud of it," I retorted.

He smiled, we laughed, I am content.

28 November 1951

Two weeks ago I wrote to my parents and told them that I was pregnant. I had great misgivings. How would they react? Would they resent the inclusion in the family of what to them might seem like a half-caste? Or would they be happy for us? What would Marianne say? Would she be jealous?

This morning we had a letter, addressed to both of us, expressing joy and concern. My mother is pleased, and that is most important to me. "I wish I could help you now," she writes, "but I cannot possibly travel. Even if I could, I would probably only be a burden." I am deeply touched. Father wants another grandson, and Marianne? She does not write anything. I feel like apologising to her that I am happy. Not only happy, but lucky the way my life has developed. Poor Marianne. I wish I could do something to renew the bond between us. Once we were so close.

6 December 1951

"Do you think we British are too reserved, even cold?" Dr Mcdonald threw the question at me, taking the stethoscope off my tummy. "We are sometimes told that foreigners consider us to be so." He had finished his monthly examination of my rotundity and sat down. I like talking with him. This question, however, made me a little suspicious, and I felt weary. What could it lead up to? I started:

"No, you are not. I know a fair number of people in this country. Reserved yes, but never cold." I winked at him. We know each other well, I felt quite free to do that. "You are an insular race and, I believe, will remain one. Celts, Chinese, Indians, Anglo-Saxons, Normans and all."

He let out a deep laugh of the belly variety.

"You cannot make an abstract summary of a race, can you?" he asked. – "You are right. We are a nation of many races. I think the Nazis made the mistake of trying to identify race and nation."

"Quite," I said. "Many of the Jews in Germany were more German than Hitler who, after all, was Austrian. The strength of a nation should lie in the combination of racial diversities and cultural unity."

"What do you mean by culture? Intellectualism?" There was doubt in his voice.

"Not necessarily," I answered. "No, I mean how we

behave, what we eat, what games we play. I mean our whole social existence. You know – and I say this only to you –" He gave me a broad smile.

"I do not think that British people on the whole are intellectuals, unlike the French and Germans. I think you rely more on instinct."

"Perhaps you are right," he replied. "The lessons of history, our own history, are in our bones. I believe Germans carry them in their heads."

I paused for a moment and then said, "Another thing is, you live on a crowded island, you protect your privacy. For that reason, until people like myself know you, you may appear cold. But look what capacity this nation has to express itself on the stage, to interpret music. The best plays, good players, wonderful musicians. There is passion, devotion. No lack of feeling there, no coldness."

"I enjoy talking to you," he said, "even if we do not solve the problems. I say, were there any other patients in the waiting room? Sorry, I got carried away."

"There may be now", I smiled. "I'll see you in four weeks time."

"Yes. And take good care. Plenty of sleep and fresh air. You'll be fine."

I walked home, thinking about our conversation. When I reported it to Dick, he remarked in a stoical fashion: "No good analysing everything. We are as we are." Typical.

"I like you as you are anyway," I laughed and hugged him.

9 December 1951

We have a television set! I am very excited. It is one of the firm's laboratory sets, on loan to Dick. We both feel we'll have to own one ourselves later, after the baby is born. There are plays, old films, sport and cartoons for the children. Joyce came over for an afternoon chat. Her four year old boy kept trying to look behind the set and, when I switched it off, he called out: "Come out then, where are you?"

It is very interesting to see news every day and on a much wider scale than cinema news – instant information, so to speak.

Stirrings of unrest in South Africa, the struggle against nuclear power, the plight of underprivileged nations. And on the home front we can now see Richard Dimbleby in his fascinating 'London Town' programme and as a personal guide through great public occasions.

I wonder: Will these pictures in the home change our lives eventually? Perhaps, as television spreads, people will not want to go out as much as at present and, maybe, cinemas will have to close. What a silly thought! Nothing can replace a good film, seen on a large screen. It could be that people will be politically better informed and educated. A whole new view of life opens up.

20 December 1951

Christmas is approaching once more.

"We ought to buy a refrigerator," Dick mumbles and speaks more to himself than to me. I prick my ears up.

"Oh yes, it is so much easier to store food, especially now, at Christmas time."

"Yes, that as well. But I was mainly thinking of the baby. Always fresh milk and orange juice. And you needn't go shopping every day."

"Can we afford it?" I asked. I know only very few people who have a refrigerator or 'fridge', as everybody is beginning to call it.

"My dear girl, if you can go and buy a piano, I might as well have a fridge. I am also thinking of cold beer for myself."

I smile. Ever so often he tries to make me feel a little guilty about that piano. It does not work. I am very happy to have it and play and even practise frequently. The refrigerator will be particularly good this Christmas. We have planned a Christmas Eve with friends and their children and they are all looking forward to a 'German evening', which means live candles on a richly decorated tree, a good supper of potato salad and Frankfurters scrounged (without coupons) from a Jewish delicatessen shop, lots of cake, a punch bowl Dick is in charge of, and presents for the children under the tree. I hope it is not going to be too boisterous.

It was not. It was absolutely perfect. We had four children in the house, their two sets of parents as well, and our Grandma. But no Roy, no Henning. I firmly refused to think about that, rang our little bell when everything in the lounge was prepared and looked at their faces. Children everywhere are the same: wondering, starry-eyed, with little shrieks of delight squatting down to look at the beautiful crib in front of the tree (a present from my parents and Marianne), grabbing the presents as I, just as I have done in the past with Roy, said: "No, first a carol or a Christmas poem." We all went through to the dining room, gathered round the piano, and their bright voices joined me in 'Silent Night'. No problem any longer with the English text of the beautiful old song.

My mother-in-law came over to me and whispered:

"You know, thinking back to the first Christmas Eve here, you were right. It is something very special. Thank you, my dear. Thank you for making us happy."

Next year, if all goes well, our own child will gaze at the Christmas candles.

"Well," I said to Dick, deeply satisfied after everybody had gone home, "that was marvellous, don't you think so?"

"Not too bad, not too bad at all," he said in his quiet fashion.

I was fuming, but held back. How often have I heard that expression as well as 'Quite nice' and, which to me is especially demoralising, 'I don't mind'. If I interpret these sayings and give them their proper definition in German, it is something like:

> not too bad = indicating 'very good, very enjoyable'
> quite nice = saying 'pleasant, (perhaps even) pretty'
> and I don't mind = 'it's all the same to me'

which, to my mind, smacks of total indifference to whatever is being suggested. Or is it a polite expression: I do not want to take the initiative? Nobody ought to be indifferent to such a degree. Do English people mean what they are saying when using these idioms? Why are they so hesitant in praising, so embarrassed about receiving compliments, and always understating?

Or, which could just be the case, am I the one who is too effusive?

27 December 1951

I am in the room we prepared weeks ago, for the events to come. My thoughts keep wandering: This is the nicest place for a birth. No fear here, but hope. Life knocking at the door. I would not want to miss a second of it. 'Every day is a new beginning, every morn is a world made new . . .' Where did I hear or read this? I do not remember, but I like it, and the rhythm of the lines is pulsating within me as I am restlessly moving about.

28 December 1951

"Would you like to go to Stratford and see a play?" Dick asked me just before Christmas.

Would I! I know it is 'History' season in the Shakespeare Theatre, and I had not yet seen any Shakespeare plays in English, with the exception of 'Hamlet' in the cinema. And if it was any 'Henry' or 'Richard', wonderful!

"It will mean a long day," he mused, "perhaps a matinee is best. And we could take Roy and Joyce, go by car."

I started looking at the Stratford programme in the 'Daily Telegraph' straightaway.

"It won't be too strenuous for you?" he worried.

"No, of course not. I'll be the lady in the back. You drive."

We have been to Stratford twice before, but not to visit the theatre. Once I got to the river, I found it is dominated by the theatre, bold, rather severe, striking in its simplicity, with the backcloth of Holy Trinity Church, where Shakespeare is buried. I still have not seen his birthplace from the inside. On both occasions when we were there, hundreds of visitors wanted to see it as well, and we do not like queuing. Still, one day. What a pleasure though, to look at the almshouses, the old Grammar School, the shop fronts which have been lovingly maintained. I have seen Anne Hathaway's cottage, that delightful timber-framed house with a thatched roof and tiny latticed windows. And the lovely, old-fashioned garden. I knew then what the meaning of an 'English garden' is. The fragrance of lavender, herbs and blossoms add to the unique charm of the garden. A perfect setting for the cottage! To me it was breathtaking and again, as so many times in London, spelt history.

We booked tickets for this afternoon: Richard III with Richard Burton as the King. I remember the plot from my schooldays, but read the play before we went. No simple matter for somebody whose native tongue is not English, to understand the wealth of Shakespeare's language.

We took Joyce and Roy, her husband, with us. I now wish I had briefed them. They might not have liked that but, as it is, they seemed bored. Roy looked half asleep throughout the play, Joyce fidgeted and was probably longing for a nice cup of tea. They were disturbing me, distracting me from an absolutely brilliant performance. Immediately, I felt guilty as well. It is our fault that we persuaded them. They perhaps did not like to say 'no'. Who, in any case, states that we all have to like Shakespeare? It could be that they both hated his plays at school and never tried to find out more about them later on. Almost at once, I rejected the fleeting thought to talk to them about it. They are such good friends; why embarrass them?

1 January 1952

Marianne was on the telephone about Mother. She is at home now. The hospital cannot help any longer.

I know she has been there for three weeks. 'An exploratory operation' we were told. I had written to my sister and asked her to keep us informed. Now she is in Marianne's care again. I know instinctively that her life is coming to an end. I ought to go and see her. Yet it is impossible for me to travel now. There are only four to five weeks to go before our child is born, I cannot risk travelling for nearly twenty-four hours. I am extremely tired as it is.

I would like to see them all, but I don't know how I can do it right now. How disloyal I feel! Perhaps I can fly? It is not feasible. It would cost far too much; I could not possibly ask Dick, especially as I know in my heart that he would not want to stop me.

I explained to Marianne what the situation was and told her how much I would like to talk to Mother. But Marianne was very cold: "That is out of the question. She is very tired and under sedation most of the time."

I was nearly in tears. I felt I could not decide anything then. I just asked Marianne: "Will you tell Mother we spoke?" I almost pleaded with her: "Will you tell her I send my love?"

There was a brief "Of course" from her before she put the receiver down.

5 January 1952

I could not go to Kiel. Doctor and husband reacted with a definite 'no'. I know mother is dying and day after day I waited and dreaded the telephone call from Kiel. When it came, I felt desperately empty, drained. The last time I saw my mother I felt that all the resentment and bitterness that had built up since the end of the war had been wiped out. We were able to talk, to understand each other and there was, in me, love for her such as I had never felt before. "Without your mother you are truly grown-up now," a voice says to me, "you will be a mother yourself soon and have to think of her grandchild."

I look again at the letters she wrote since she knew of my pregnancy, touching letters, talking of a new bond and hope for the future through the child. One part of my life has gone for ever now. What will the next years hold?

Dick watches me: "Come on, love. We have so much to live for, and she will have the peace she longed for. I'll put some music on for you. She loved music, like you do."

How is it he always seems to know my needs?

"There. Your favourite symphony. And remember, I am here."

The first bars fill the room, he comes over to me and dries my tears.

15 January, 1952

Marianne wrote and told us that they buried my mother in a small, beautiful cemetery outside Kiel, close to the sea she had loved so much. Father is heartbroken and is losing his sense of reality. He has begun to call my sister 'mother'. How sad that is. Perhaps this will change after a while; he has always been so fond of living. Surely in spring I should be able to go to him and show him his grandchild? But spring is a long time away.

20 January 1952

How strange this is: I have been in England now for over four years and, most of the time, I think in English. I dream in English as well. And yet, I am suddenly stunned when Dick catches me checking the grocery bill.

"What are you doing? Mumbling away?"

"I simply want to find out where all the money went," I replied.

"Yes, but you do it in German," he said.

I froze.

"You are right." I reacted quickly. "How odd, I don't think I can do it in English. I mean, automatically do it."

Up to that point I had never thought about it. I was very puzzled and started wondering. It is true. My immediate reaction to almost everything is in English. I can claim to be bilingual, but not when it comes to sums. There is a blind spot. Why is that so? And not when it concerns measurements either. I still have to think: a yard means not quite a metre: an inch means 2.5cm. Why? Could it be that the art of counting is one of the first things small children learn? And it stays with them for ever in their native language? They acquire it long before they are able to read, so it becomes a habit that is hard, perhaps even impossible, to break. It requires a very conscious effort to deal with figures in a foreign language. I must watch myself in future and, yes, I must find out if other 'aliens' have the same experience.

22 January 1952

Going to the West End to see a play in one of London's many theatres is becoming very tiring and strenuous for me. Instead, we are regular visitors to the local cinemas. One is within walking distance of our house, and it is such a pleasure to walk home through the park, talking of the film we have seen. Dick is very critical, sometimes a little cynical, trying to convince me of the improbability of it all. I am forever romantic, optimistic, even believing. This is a whole new world for me, with old British and American films we in Germany never had a chance to see. They were forbidden. Fred Astaire and Ginger Rogers dancing, Vivien Leigh and Clark Gable in 'Gone with the Wind' – unforgettable! And Laurence Oliver as 'Hamlet'. Shakespeare on the picture screen, what an event. Until Dick gently pointed out that there had been other films in earlier years, created from Shakespeare's plays.

Films in pre-war Germany and the few new ones during the war were filled with political propaganda of that time, or were concerned with Prussian history and its leaders, such as 'Frederic the Great' or 'Scharnhorst'. They were brilliantly conceived and executed, but never showed us much of real life. Margaret Lockwood's 'Wicked Lady' in contrast, the highway woman and rebel against tradition, boredom, husband and friends, – unthinkable in the Germany of my time (She has to be punished, though!). I like English films with honest, forceful scenes of dreary East End life where, nevertheless, indestructable Cockney humour is always shining through.

The cinema holds me from the moment we have paid our one shilling and ninepence for a seat in the stalls and are sitting down, I with a short backward glance at the courting seats – cosy double seats in the back – which I find amusing, time and time again. Then on to the Pathe News and two absorbing films. Two! I have never been used to that. The interval between them is punctuated by the sound of the mighty Wurlitzer organ, as its player appears from out of the floor, seated at the controls, and for about fifteen minutes plays popular tunes. That at least reminds me of Germany: Organ play before the start of the film. However, the German Organist did not pop up from nowhere, like Jack-in-the-box.

The films over, everybody stands and listens to the National Anthem. Dick had to nudge me the first time we visited a cinema together. "Get up," he whispered.

How odd, I thought then. Now I realise that the British, though undemonstrative, even shy in showing their loyalties, have a deep-rooted feeling for their King, and many of them for their new Prime Minister, judging by his reception when cinema-goers watch the Pathe News. Churchill has been the Prime Minister again for some months now, his first peacetime administration.

Gradually, rationing is easing up a little (although I still think we have enough of everything), the employment level is better. The Welfare State with the National Health Service remains. I like that. It was brilliantly conceived, and the aim of the scheme is admirable. I suppose Churchill and his new Government recognise this as well. Auntie Rose, however, does not agree and states that she will never join it. For the first time since the war ended it looks as if life is going to be easier for everybody.

24 January 1952

These weeks, waiting for our baby, I read avidly. I do not like knitting now; memories of endless 'undoings' of old pullovers and cardigans during the war, to create something new for Henning and his cousin Wolfgang out of hard, itchy wool, have taken away my taste for that type of activity. Probably forever. Anyway, there are aunts and cousins in my new family who apparently love doing it for me. I accept shamelessly and read, not with too much discretion, but anything from Kipling to Monica Dickens and Nevil Shute, from Shelley to Tennyson. And biographies, both in German and English. Dick belongs to 'The Book Club' and will always ask me what I would like.

How good the local libraries are! I watch people literally loading up with books on a Saturday afternoon. It does not cost a penny either and is really marvellous. Perhaps they buy fewer books here than in Germany? Most Germans love to own books, and it is quite important to display them in their flats or houses. Possessions, to show your status, are essential.

From my last visit to Kiel I have come back with some German books. I did not have any before that, with the exception of an old dictionary. Now they are proudly arranged in 'my' corner, close to my favourite armchair: the old loved ones of my formative years, such as Goethe, Kleist, Rilke and Thomas Mann, whose novels had been banned during the Nazi era, but which one can again buy freely in Germany. From now on I shall always ask for German books, if my family should want to give me a present.

13 February 1952

Dawn. I am awake, very frightened and with the startled feeling as though someone had put their hands on me and roughly disturbed me. I am lying very still, my heart beating wildly, wide-open eyes fixed on the window, pale in early light. There is that touch again. This time it becomes a sharp pain, stabbing. Sweat breaks out on my forehead. Suddenly it is all over. Perhaps a false alarm, but I want to be ready, mentally prepared.

I look across to the cradle. It has been in Dick's family for a long time; he slept and dreamt in it during the first months of his life, and so have all four of Auntie Rose's children. I leave my bed, go over and gently rock it. Everything is as it should be: clean sheets, a handknitted bedcover, a shawl – all in white. Boy or girl? Now I just have to wait.

I move across to the window, open the curtains wide and glimpse the first snow of the year slowly, silently settling on the lawn below. It is a grey, grey winter morning, but my heart begins to sing. I am supremely happy, waiting for our child in our own home. The house seems to speak to me, reassure me. There are echoes of footsteps – footsteps to come. Unborn voices too.

I must write down what I feel this very moment. It will never happen again. I shall want to talk to our child about it, I want to be aware of every second before the baby's birth. Later there will not be much time to record events.

But, oh, this sudden gripping devastating pain once more!

I must call Dick.

14 February 1952

Our little Victor is asleep in the cradle beside me. He is so perfect. And so big! Nine pounds twelve ounces.

Looking back, the last few hours before the birth were very busy, and very funny too. I called Dick when the pains came back. The minutes that followed were filled with panic. Dick couldn't find his trousers – which he insisted on doing – or the light switch. And all he needed to do was to go downstairs and make a phone call.

Eventually both Doctor McDonald and Nurse Bedford arrived. She had two main concerns: she wanted a cup of tea and wanted to watch King George's lying-in-state on television. She was taken aback when she heard that we did not have a set (the borrowed one went back weeks ago). She seemed to be horrified at the idea that it would take many hours for the baby to be born.

Dick kept opening the door now and again. He could not bear to be present, but could not help not being there either. Half past one in the afternoon and it was all over, so both doctor and nurse were able to go home and watch television.

Welcome to life, Victor. The name seems to us the most appropriate for a child who has come into our world helping to join two nations that have been at war so often, and are now trying to build up a safe future for both.

I slept for quite a while and was woken up by Dick, who came in with a bunch of roses. When Henning was born his father had brought me flowers too, but everything was different and cold. I felt terribly lonely then, in an expensive private clinic. But now I am in my own bed, being looked after by the man I love.

Dick is not a man of many words, and the ones he has managed to put in writing today have been the most special ever. Together with the flowers there was a plain white card. The hand-written words read:

Today on this earthly stage
you have turned another page.
The play continues its exciting run,
it's time for triumph, time for fun.
Carry on in the leading part,
you've always played it well from start.
You may say whate'er you will:
For me you'll always head the bill.

I sank back under the blankets, feeling gloriously happy. Later he came in with a tray, complete with serviette, a flower, two golden eggs on toast (my favourite), a glass of champagne, and the broadest smile in his face. I love my *chef,* who put it all down and said: "I hope you'll enjoy it."

All I could say was: "Thank you. Thank you for everything. Right now my world is perfect."

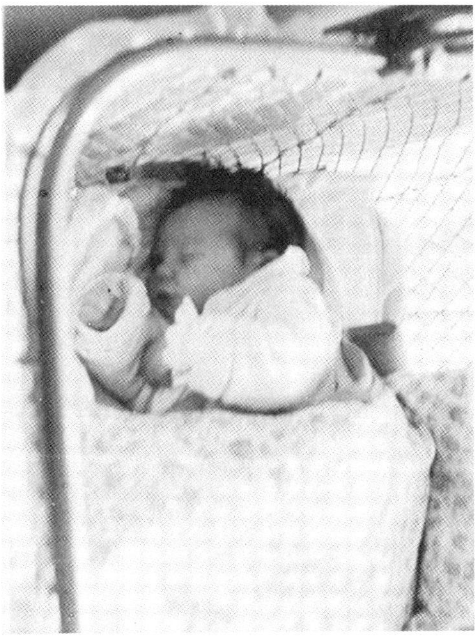

Epilogue

Am I really as I appear in the book? In some instances, I hope not. I do not always like myself.

Some of the people mentioned are no longer with us, others have grown old, like myself. But then, the book ought to be read less for what I personally experienced than for what that particular time offered to me and how I reacted.

There was a lot of hope in those years for a new kind of world, for a peaceful relationship between nations. Reality, however, does not always keep up with expectations.

Many of my personal hopes have come to fruition. Money has not always been plentiful, indeed, at times it has been remarkably short. It did not matter. I have never forgotten the post-war years withouth warmth, food and material goods. I, together with thousands of people, learned to cope, to survive.

Eventually, our family numbered five: ourselves and three boys who surprised us at times with their understanding of teamship in the family. We are very proud of them, and always included in our thoughts are the other two sons: Roy, whom we lost to his mother and who has made a career in Australia, and Henning, who made a name for himself in German Television, the theatre and journalism. I fulfilled my dream of teaching.

Our children love going to Germany – as tourists. And they behave like visitors: two of them using the language, albeit not fluently, the third one restricting himself to the minimum of polite expressions, making up for it with his father's shy smile. Although only one generation removed, they do not see their roots in my old country; they are sympathetic towards my own past, but in the end shrug off what they know of it. There is a strong tendency to say: "Come on, let's go home now. We do not belong here."

At one point, due to an unfortunate business association, we lost a lot of money and our home. A fresh start for my husband, offered by a friend, brought us to Malvern and we found what so many English people dream about: a very old cottage with a beautiful garden. Never mind that it was not much more than a ruin at that time. The boys looked over the old Malvern stone wall into the terraced garden and shouted: "This it is!" I was horrified. I saw years of work ahead. In the end, I was wrong. It has become a haven, a home for the evergrowing family, in the same way as my adopted country has given me new roots.